Direct
Action

JAMES TRACY

Direct
Action

RADICAL PACIFISM
FROM THE UNION EIGHT
TO THE CHICAGO SEVEN

UNIVERSITY OF CHICAGO PRESS
Chicago & London

JAMES TRACY received his Ph.D. from Stanford University. While completing this book, he was Residential Scholar at The Hotchkiss School and a Visiting Fellow at Yale University.

The University of Chicago Press, Chicago 60637
The University of Chicago Press, Ltd., London
©1996 by The University of Chicago
All rights reserved. Published 1996
Printed in the United States of America
05 04 03 02 01 00 99 98 97 96   1 2 3 4 5

ISBN: 0-226-81127-1 (cloth)
       0-226-81130-1 (paper)

Library of Congress Cataloging-in-Publication Data

Tracy, James.
    Direct action : radical pacifism from the Union Eight to the
Chicago Seven / James Tracy.
        p.   cm.
    Includes bibliographical references and index.
    1. Passive resistance—United States—History.   2. Pacifists—
United States—History.   3. Direct action—History.   I. Title.
HM278.T73   1996
303.6′1—dc20   96-12278
                                                          CIP

⊗The paper used in this publication meets the minimum requirements of the American National Standard for Information Sciences—Permanence of Paper for Printed Library Materials, ANSI Z39.48-1984.

THIS BOOK IS DEDICATED TO MY MENTORS,
ESTELLE FREEDMAN AND PAUL FALER

AND TO BAYARD RUSTIN,
WHO GAVE AS MUCH AS ANY
AND FORGAVE MORE THAN MOST

Contents

Acknowledgments

In the course of researching and writing this book, I received invaluable help from many people. This project has made me appreciate as never before the extent to which historical writing arises from a community of scholars. More people helped with this book than I can possibly mention here, but the following deserve special thanks.

Estelle Freedman of Stanford University has continued to share her enthusiasm and wisdom long after the demands of dissertation advising were met. Thanks, also, to George Fredrickson, Paul Seaver, and David Kennedy of Stanford.

While completing this book, I was fortunate to be Residential Scholar at The Hotchkiss School and Visiting Fellow in the Department of History at Yale University. I am very grateful to both of these institutions. While at Yale, conversing with John Demos helped clarify my thinking about the craft of narrative history, while my participation in the interdisciplinary Religious

Institutions and Society Workshop provided valuable input. I am especially grateful to Rob Oden, now president of Kenyon College, for his support.

The following people showed enormous generosity of time and spirit by reading and commenting upon all or sizable portions of the book manuscript: Stewart Burns, David Dellinger, Estelle Freedman, Staughton Lynd, Janet Sargent, and Lawrence S. Wittner. Also of inestimable value were the anonymous comments of the readers for the University of Chicago Press and the sagacious help given by my editor, Douglas Mitchell, and his associate, Matt Howard. Long conversations about cinema with Doug have been unexpected delights along the way.

My hearty thanks to the following activists who took the time to explain to me their personal experience within this history: Tom Cornell, Dave Dellinger, Ralph DiGia, George Houser, Staughton Lynd, Brad Lyttle, Dave McReynolds, Ira Sandperl, Bill Sutherland, and Marjorie Swann. Getting to know these people has been the most rewarding aspect of my research.

I have received the patient assistance of more librarians and archivists than I can count, but especially noteworthy have been Jim Knox of Stanford University; Wendy E. Chmielewski and her fine staff at the Swarthmore College Peace Collection; Scott Kennedy, director of the Kepler Library and Resource Center for Nonviolence in Santa Cruz, California; Bev Hoffman and Walter DeMelle of Hotchkiss; and Marjorie Ciarlante and her colleagues at the National Archives.

Thanks, also, to Noel Hartman for his help as research assistant; David Dellinger, Dorothy Marder, Diana Davies, Walter Neagle, Robert F. Haiko, and Ruth Benn for their assistance with photos; Sisters Rosemarie Greco, D.W., and Jo-Ann Iannotti, O.P., of Wisdom House for organizing such fine programs and for allowing me to use their facilities to interview Tom Cornell; and Dick Bunce of Pacifica National Office.

Finally, I would like to express my deep appreciation to my parents for encouraging me to see learning as a means to fuller life. As for my wife, Janet, and my son, Forrest, I cannot find adequate words to express what the love we have shared through the years has meant to me. There is a picture of Forrest cradled in Janet's arms. Here now is this extraordinary young man towering over his mother.

Introduction

In the 1940s, a small but dauntless movement, whose adherents termed themselves "radical pacifists," emerged out of the conscientious objector population of World War II. Between 1940 and 1970, these radical pacifists became the principal interpreters of Gandhism on the American Left. Despite its small size, their movement made an enormous impact on postwar American dissent. Groups such as the Congress of Racial Equality, the War Resisters League, the Fellowship of Reconciliation, and the Committee for Nonviolent Action played key roles in determining the tactics, structure, and culture of the postwar Left. These groups would stamp postwar American dissent with certain characteristics: a tactical commitment to direct action; an agenda that posited race and militarism (instead of labor) as the central social issues in the United States; an experimental protest style that emphasized media-savvy, symbolic confrontation with institutions deemed oppressive; an ethos that privileged action over analysis and extolled nonviolent individual resistance, especially when it involved "putting one's body on the line"; and an organizational structure that was nonhierarchical, decentralized, and oriented toward concensus decision making. Genealogies of the Civil Rights, antiwar, and antinuclear movements in this period are incomplete without understanding the history of radical pacifism.

Part of the explanation for the disproportionate influence this small movement exerted upon the culture of postwar political dissent is that radical pacifists touched in a distinctive way upon a growing ambivalence Americans felt about the implications of the Cold War for democracy. Radical pacifists were, at root, radical libertarians, attempting to reassert autonomous individualism amidst modern mass society. This orientation made them particularly sensitive to all forms of authoritarianism. Their forms of protest, which explicitly and implicitly hearkened back to nineteenth-century ideals of American individualism, resonated with increasing numbers of people in the postwar period.

Along with their influence on the American political tradition, radical pacifists provide intriguing personal histories, replete with tales of courage, commitment, heroic struggle against remarkable odds, and tragedy. The people who led radical pacifism—such as Dave Dellinger, A. J. Muste, and Bayard Rustin—seasoned its history with their inimitable styles. In order to effectively portray the people who made this history, I have written this book as a collective biography in narrative form. This format helps to bring out the drama of the passionate struggles of radical pacifists to transform America over the course of three decades, amid innumerable contingencies.

The full history of radical pacifism, however, is not a triumphant one. In the 1940s and 1950s, radical pacifists developed a protest style that was, of necessity, tailored to small groups of activists. One of their most impressive accomplishments was that they intrepidly remained active at the height of the Cold War and the Red Scare. Yet the tactics and ethos that suited small groups calling out in the political wilderness of the 1940s and 1950s were not particularly apt for the mass-based movements that emerged in the 1960s. Radical pacifism's influence upon the foundations of the new radicalism, I argue, was both a major reason for the powerful symbolism of public protest during the late 1950s and 1960s and a key contributory factor in the ultimate unraveling of the Left in the late 1960s. Radical pacifism, in short, was better suited for symbolic activism engaged in by small groups than for the instrumentalist work of building sustainable mass movements. The history of radical pacifism, then, has explanative value for the course taken by the American Left during and after the 1960s. It also reveals at once the strengths and limitations of American individualism. For this reason, the history of radical pacifism is instructive for both the Left and the Right in America.

One

FELONS

The photograph picked up by newspapers across the country in 1940 showed eight young men sitting on opposing benches in a police wagon about to convey them to federal prison. Their appearance contrasted with their setting: well-groomed and wearing suits and ties, the men could be taken for sitting on church pews if it were not for the handcuffs and barred window. They looked determined but not grim. On the same day that this picture was taken, November 14, 1940, Reinhold Niebuhr, the most prominent theologian of the time, delivered a sermon denouncing their criminal behavior.[1] What had these felons done to warrant such attention?

The "Union Eight" were a group of students at Union Theological Seminary whose crime was a refusal to acknowledge the conscripting power of the state.[2] In 1940, when the United States government passed the first peacetime military draft in its history, twenty students preparing for the ministry at   1

Union announced their refusal to register with Selective Service. Eventually, twelve changed their minds under intense pressure from teachers at Union (including Niebuhr), parents, and many leaders of national pacifist organizations. Eight of the original twenty, however, persisted in resisting any compliance with the conscription law. By doing so, they chose imprisonment at a federal penitentiary over the automatic conscientious objection exemption available to seminarians.

"I have every appreciation for the integrity of our eight young men," Niebuhr wrote four days after their arrest, "but I do not see how they can be helped when in effect they courted martyrdom in the hope that their situation would start a general movement in the country." Niebuhr noted that he knew "some of these boys very intimately" and had "talked the matter over with them at length." Yet in the end he could neither change their minds nor support them: "I do not feel that they are contending for the right of the Christian to abstain from war," he wrote. "They take the position that the conscription law is itself totalitarian. . . . I cannot honestly support them in essentially anarchistic philosophies of government."[3]

Niebuhr's summation showed a clear understanding of the Union Eight's analysis and intentions. The men did, indeed, hope to start a general movement, one of "extreme libertarianism" against the coercive power of the United States government, which they felt was marching in lockstep toward fascism.[4] A week before the draft took effect, they issued a joint statement that read, in part: "We have . . . been led to our conclusion on the conscription law in the light of its totalitarian nature. . . . We believe, therefore, that by opposing the Selective Service law, we will be striking at the heart of totalitarianism as well as war."[5]

While by any objective criteria World War II was not the heyday of pacifism, for young militants in the pacifist community the war years were filled with an exhilarating sense of discovery and hope. The Union Eight were the catalysts and leaders of a new radical pacifist movement that was forged during World War II in the Civilian Public Service (CPS) camps the government established for registered conscientious objectors (C.O.s) and in the federal prisons where the government placed those, like the Union Eight, who refused to register or did not otherwise meet its criteria for C.O. status. These young men were confident that they were the founders of a new revolution that would redeem American social relations by means of a combative and creative nonviolence. One of them, Roy Finch, would neatly summarize the confident belligerence of these Young Turks in the 1940s: "We have to assimilate the idea of fighting to the idea of pacifism," Finch wrote. "We want more and not less militancy, more controversy, more negativism, more open conflict."[6]

In the conscientious objector communities of World War II, radical pacifism coalesced as a movement around the charismatic leadership of a few young men: Roy Finch, George Houser, Bayard Rustin, Jim Peck, and, especially, Dave Dellinger. Dellinger was older than many of the other C.O.s during the war, turning twenty-five in 1940, and more advanced in his thinking about the revolutionary role he felt libertarian nonviolence should play in redeeming Western society. Like others of the Union Eight, Dellinger had traveled many passionate political and spiritual paths before arriving in that police wagon in November 1940.

BACKGROUND

In many ways, Dellinger's socioeconomic background and the political experiences in the 1930s that prepared the ground for his 1940s radicalism were typical of most other young men who became radical pacifists. Dellinger was born in 1915 to a blue-blood Massachusetts family whose American pedigree stretched back to before the Revolution. His father was a prominent Boston lawyer who counted Calvin Coolidge among his friends.

Dellinger enjoyed the privileges of an elite education. After graduating from high school at the age of sixteen, he attended Yale and later studied at Oxford on fellowship.

While at Yale, Dellinger participated in the intellectual ferment of the 1930s, struggling with the political and social implications of the Depression. He developed a friendship with fellow student W. W. Rostow, who later became a key adviser to Presidents Kennedy and Johnson on the conduct of the Vietnam War. Dellinger's time at Oxford during the 1936–1937 academic year, however, was especially transformative. During that time, he traveled to Nazi-dominated Germany, often opting to stay at bed-and-breakfasts in the Jewish quarters of cities. Dellinger was appalled by this firsthand experience with fascism, but he also felt increasingly frustrated by the ineffectual response of Western democracies to the fascist threat. In September of 1936, Dellinger traveled behind the Loyalist lines of the Spanish Civil War. He was so moved by the republican resistance to superior fascist forces that he considered taking up a gun to help, but he decided instead that violence was a futile method. He would later write that "the peasants and some of the soldiers . . . were the most inspiring people I had ever met, and I knew then that I would always be a revolutionary . . . but a nonviolent revolutionary, because the other way is tempting but doesn't work."[7]

Upon his return to the United States, Dellinger moved back to New Haven, auditing courses at Yale Divinity School until, in 1939, he entered Union Theological Seminary. At that time, Union was both the bastion of liberal theology and the pinnacle of neo-Orthodox thought in the country. Union's approach was still heavily influenced by the Social Gospel tradition, of which Walter Rauschenbusch had been the major exponent. This theology, which emerged in part from Rauschenbusch's efforts to feed and house New York City's impoverished immigrants in the late nineteenth century, offered an optimistic appraisal of the human capacity for good and the perfectibility of society through reform. In 1939, however, Union was also home to Paul Tillich and Reinhold Niebuhr. Niebuhr had once been strongly influenced by Rauschenbusch. In fact, Niebuhr had been executive secretary in the early 1930s of the Fellowship of Reconciliation, a large pacifist organization steeped in Social Gospel assumptions. By the late 1930s, however, Niebuhr had rejected the Social Gospel's assumption that evil is an aberration in the human condition and had instead become the foremost theologian of "Christian Realism." By Christian Realism, Niebuhr meant that Christians should recognize that evil will be an ineradicable part of the human condition until the arrival of the Kingdom of God. He therefore posited the need for interim ethics, while awaiting the Kingdom, that required Christians to make moral compromises in an imperfect world, such as using violence to effect a positive end. As World War II began, therefore, Niebuhr argued that pacifism was irrelevant to the struggle against fascism.

Dellinger quickly established himself as a magnetic leader among a segment of Union's seminarians. In his first year, he became the president of his class and joined a group of students, including two who would later be among the Union Eight, in an intentional community in Harlem they dubbed the "Harlem Commune." Most of the students residing in the commune were whites from comfortable middle-class backgrounds who had been raised in a liberal Christian tradition and had had varying degrees of contact with the Marxist Left during the 1930s. These students modeled their pacifism on Mohandas Gandhi, who had established "ashrams" in India as communal bases for political and spiritual renewal. Gandhi was at that time leading a massive nonviolent campaign against British rule in India. Using a creative combination of dramatic individual acts, such as hunger strikes, to embarrass his adversaries and mass-scale civil disobedience to coerce concessions from the British, Gandhi practiced nonviolence as an active force capable of revolutionizing unjust social orders.[8] This intrigued young pacifists in the United States who were seeking to redefine pacifism as a social force potent enough to provide a viable alternative to waging war against Hitler.

Virtually every major formative influence on their political sensibilities led those who lived at the Harlem Commune to

assume that race was a central moral issue in American society. Belief in racial equality was a central tenet of the Social
Gospel tradition in which many of the ashram's residents
had been reared.[9] Gandhi had raised the issue of racism in his
critiques of Western colonialism and in his struggles to gain
social acceptance for Untouchables within Indian society.
The Marxist Left had also made racial injustice a focus of its
organizing efforts, most notably when the Communist party
(CP-USA) made the defense of the Scottsboro Boys a cause
celebre.[10]

It was natural, then, for this predominantly white group of
theology students to select Harlem as the site for their community. In late 1939, they moved to a new commune that Dellinger
founded in a blighted section of Newark. This "Newark
Ashram" would become a base for many resisting conscription
during the Second World War. Bill Sutherland, an African-
American who joined the Newark Ashram due to Dellinger's
influence, recalls that during the war there was a "constant turn-
over" of the community's residents "as the FBI came in and
took us away."[11]

1940 was a bad year for pacifism. As Americans looked uneas-
ily at the military conflicts raging in Asia and Europe, pacifist
sentiment became the reserve of a miniscule minority. Things
had seemed much different just a few years before. In the early
and mid-1930s, when the economic concerns of the Depression
were paramount and war seemed a distant possibility, a facile
pacifism had been a popular sentiment to espouse, especially
among those on the Left. Fueled in part by a revisionist disenchantment with World War I and influenced by labor's insistence that international war was antithetical to the interests of
workers, the young were especially vocal about their ostensible
pacifism in the early 1930s. In 1935, for instance, sixty thousand
college students across the country participated in a strike against
war.[12] Tens of thousands of American students emulated their
British counterparts in taking what was known as the Oxford

Pledge, committing themselves to an absolute refusal to participate in future wars.

As war loomed ever more threateningly on America's hori-
zon in the late 1930s, much of this sunshine pacifism changed
to isolationism, an antiwar sentiment that was more deeply em-
bedded in the American tradition. A survey conducted by Howard Bell showed that by 1938 American youth had shifted from
a pacifist stance to a position consistent with isolationism.
America's young people now believed that the United States
should avoid foreign entanglements, but they were willing to
fight a defensive war should it become necessary. Bell found that
over 60 percent of young men and women regarded war as a
"needless and preventable occurrence," but that over 80 percent
of males said they would fight if America were threatened with
invasion. Only about 12 percent said they would resist a future
draft. Bell was surprised by the numbers willing to fight, considering the strength of pacifism during the early 1930s—or, as he
put it, given that "probably no generation in the history of
America has been so continuously and persistently bombarded
with antiwar propaganda as the one we are studying."[13]

Bell's findings among youth were consistent with the emergence of a new isolationism across all age groups by the late
1930s that eclipsed the earlier pacifism. Membership in isolationist groups such as the America First Committee surged at
the same time that pacifist groups declined. America First was
at once opposed to United States entry into a foreign war and
in favor of a military build-up to ensure war preparedness if
military conflict became unavoidable, a kind of isolationist jin-
goism. America First also brought a paranoid style to its politics,
arguing that Roosevelt, Jews, and Anglophiles were conspiring
to steer the nation into war to satisfy their own designs. Far
from being a marginal crackpot organization, however, America
First enjoyed a mass base in those Father Coughlin years, and it
counted among its leaders Arthur Vandenberg, Senator Robert
La Follette, Jr., and, of course, Charles Lindbergh, the organization's standard-bearer.

Pacifists were caught in a bind by these developments. Only

a small fraction of the population in the country considered themselves pacifists at the time, but a large bloc of antiwar sentiment of a sort was being galvanized by events abroad. Although many pacifists felt tempted to work with America First as the only organization capable of keeping the United States out of war, most eventually decided to steer clear of such an alliance.

President Roosevelt, who had long since decided that it was in the vital interests of the United States to enter what would become World War II, felt enough pressure from the isolationist camp during his reelection bid of 1940 to disingenuously declare: "I have said this before, but I shall say it again. Your boys are not going to be sent into any foreign wars. They are going into training to form a force so strong that, by its very existence, it will keep the threat of war away from our shores."[14] While riding isolationist opinion in an election year, Roosevelt shrewdly harnessed such sentiment in support of his attempts to enhance the country's military readiness. Part of Roosevelt's program for military preparedness prior to Pearl Harbor was the passage in 1940 of the first military draft the nation had ever initiated during peacetime. Also unprecedented in this draft was the fact that Dellinger and his fellow seminarians were eligible for automatic exemption from military service if they registered with Selective Service as divinity students.

The terms of this exemption had been worked out during negotiations between the Roosevelt administration and leaders of the three largest churches that embrace pacifism as a tenet of their faith, known as the Historic Peace Churches (the Mennonites, the Brethren, and the Friends [or Quakers]). The members of the Peace Churches were determined not to repeat their experience of the previous war. When Wilson had suddenly implemented the country's first efficient draft in 1917, the Peace Churches found themselves ineffectually scrambling for legislation to protect conscientious objectors. The churches were hampered by failure to coordinate their efforts and by the lack of a viable precedent, since the Civil War draft had been implemented in such a spotty manner that pacifists had had little trouble avoiding it.[15] As a result, the Peace Churches found themselves subject to the vagaries of government officials during World War I. Despite a limited C.O. provision in the Selective Training Act of 1917, for instance, the churches were distressed to learn in August of that year that all draftees would be considered members of the military and that C.O.s were being placed in army-run camps. Once in the camps, despite orders to treat C.O.s with consideration, abuses took place with regularity. Some C.O.s reported being hung by their hands for long periods.[16]

This harrowing experience emboldened the three major Peace Churches to overcome their cultural differences sufficiently to lobby as a united front for more adequate C.O. protections when a renewed draft appeared likely in the late 1930s. The result was a model of well-coordinated, focused lobbying on behalf of a minority interest in sharp contrast to the decentralized, episodic efforts of 1917. The Selective Training and Service Act signed into law on September 16, 1940, incorporated what many Peace Church members hailed as vast improvements in C.O. provisions.

Although the government insisted on making religious opposition to all wars the sole basis for granting C.O. status, the act for the first time allowed such religious qualification by individuals who were not members of the Historic Peace Churches. More important, the act provided for the establishment of camps for C.O.s to be managed by the Peace Churches, where, in the language of the act, the men were to do "work of national importance." Even the funding for the camps was to be borne by the churches—a heavy financial burden for these small denominations, but a point the churches had themselves insisted upon to ensure more autonomy in running camp affairs.

There were, on the other hand, significant compromises in the plans for these Civilian Public Service (CPS) camps. For one thing, the act did not protect those who were opposed to war for philosophical rather than religious reasons or those who opposed particular wars rather than all wars. Nor did it protect those, known as absolutists, who were morally opposed to registering with Selective Service. By contrast, wartime Britain

allowed absolutists who refused to cooperate with the conscription system to carry on their civilian lives. There were also
basic material inadequacies in the CPS plan. Foremost among
these was that C.O.s who labored in the homefront CPS camps
received no pay. This seemed a marginal matter when the first
C.O.s were sent to camps for a year during the peacetime draft
of 1940, but, after American entrance into the war, C.O.s found
themselves held in the camps indefinitely. Those who had families to support were especially hard hit.

Despite these compromises that foreboded trouble, the
Peace Churches in 1940 hailed CPS as an important victory
that would protect their young men from religious persecution.
Many in the Peace Churches, too, were determined to make
the CPS experiment work, in part to show that they were responsible and loyal citizens despite their unpopular pacifist
stance.

To Dellinger, CPS was a "bribe" offering C.O.s security in
exchange for political quiescence.[17] He and the other members
of the Union Eight refused to register for the automatic military
exemption accorded seminarians. Instead, they issued their joint
statement condemning the conscription system as nascent fascism. This linkage, which would become central to the radical
pacifist movement that developed during World War II, arose
from a strong individualist strain among many young C.O.s,
who viewed all statism with the utmost skepticism. For the
Union Eight, the government's decision to conscript people
during peacetime, in preparation for "total war" mobilization,
was a step on the path to totalitarianism. "It is a totalitarian move
when our government insists that the manpower of the nation
take a year of military training," declared the seminarians. "It is
a totalitarian move for the president of the nation to be able
to conscript industry to produce certain materials which are
deemed necessary for national defense. . . . [In] learning to fight
American Hitlerism we will show an increasing group of war-
disillusioned Americans how to resist foreign Hitlers as well."[18]

Each of the Union Eight received enormous pressure to
comply with the new Selective Service provisions (though none

as much as Dellinger, whose conservative father threatened to commit suicide if he persisted in his absolutism).[19] Pacifist leaders urged the men to cooperate with the hard-won CPS provisions.[20] Clarence Pickett, head of the American Friends Service Committee, offered Dellinger a job as director of one of the CPS camps if he would register and seek C.O. status. But to Dellinger and his fellow radicals from Union, the CPS system was part and parcel of a new totalitarianism that depended as much upon a fully mobilized and smoothly running home front to wage war as upon its soldiers in the field. The proper response to avoid complicity, they felt, was active resistance to all the war-making functions of the state, including conscription.

On November 14, 1940, the Union Eight were carted off, *sentenced* handcuffed, under sentence to serve a year and a day at the federal penitentiary in Danbury, Connecticut, for Selective Service violations. They were the most radical and perhaps the most isolated pacifists in the country that day. But they burned with a zeal to make their incarceration a laboratory for experimenting with the tactics of a new pacifism robust enough to challenge authoritarianism in all its forms and, in so doing, to revolutionize American society.

Two

FORGING A NEW RADICALISM:
CONSCIENTIOUS OBJECTORS
DURING WORLD WAR II

CIVILIAN PUBLIC SERVICE AND PRISON

The Union Eight and others resisting the peacetime draft wasted little time disrupting their new prison settings in an attempt to experiment with nonviolent resistance to authoritarian structures. The first prison strike of the draft period began at Danbury on April 23, 1941. That day, sixteen C.O.s, including most of the Union Eight, refused to eat or work after the warden denied them permission to hold an antiwar demonstration in the prison. They also brought forth demands for desegregating the prison facilities. The punishment was confinement to their cells.[1] Harold Schoenfeld, who was a C.O. in Danbury at the time because his pacifism stemmed from socialist rather than religious conviction, recalls that the warden "was a liberal with a position of authority in an evil system. On the whole he attempted to use his authority to alleviate the evil. . . . His fate was to discover us unmanageable. We were a proud, stiff-necked lot who openly boasted we were the most radical men in the country. We lined up that way, radical versus liberal, and began our struggle."[2]

The Second World War was the formative watershed that galvanized radical pacifism into a coherent movement. Separated from the general population in their CPS camps or federal prisons, young male C.O.s lived under unique conditions of demographic density and emotional intensity they would never have encountered during peacetime. In these artificial communities, they feverishly exchanged ideas about reforging pacifism and experimented with resistance against the microcosm of the state they had near at hand in their places of internment. Most C.O.s during World War II did not join the emerging radical pacifist movement, but an influential minority in the camps and prisons found their internment during the war a radicalizing experience. Looking beyond at a world aflame, they were convinced that Western civilization was committing suicide. Many, too, concluded that the United States government, which was waging total war and had made the crucial moral decision to conduct strategic bombing, was on an evolutionary path toward totalitarianism. Like-minded draft-age men began to coalesce around young militants such as Dellinger who entered the war with a well-articulated desire to retool nonviolence as a coercive resistance method capable of disrupting the workings of authoritarian structures and righting social injustice.

By the end of the war, a distinct radical pacifist program claimed adherents in prisons and CPS camps across the country who exchanged information and ideas by a variety of networks. The accident of its birth in these C.O. prison and camp populations would stamp radical pacifism with certain characteristics. Radical pacifists, for instance, concluded that the modern state, even in the United States, gravitated by its very nature toward becoming a vast prison camp, and so their program focused on reasserting political space for autonomous individuals by symbolic acts of resistance, an agenda that would prove remarkably disruptive to the government's handling of C.O.s during the war.

Between 1941 and 1947, the federal government established 151 CPS camps, spread across the country from Roseburg, Oregon, to Gainesville, Florida, to house those C.O.s who cooperated with Selective Service. The total number of men placed in CPS during the war years was 11,996.[3] Most of those in CPS were members of the three major Peace Churches: 4,665 Mennonites, 1,353 from the Church of the Brethren, and 951 Friends (or Quakers). A welter of over two hundred other denominations were represented under the new religious exemptions, including one Taoist, one Rosicrucian, and two Zoroastrians.[4]

The three Historic Peace Churches felt that their traditions were too distinct to attempt unified camps, so they ran separate camps for their own members. At the outset of the war, these were the only three choices in CPS, so those assigned to CPS from other denominations had to choose a Peace Church under whose rule they preferred to live. Because the Friends were generally viewed as the most worldly and politically engaged of the three, they initially received the bulk of those entering CPS from traditions outside the Peace Churches, including many of the most political, such as the forty-six men who designated their religious denomination as the War Resisters League. During the course of the war, some Methodist-run camps were established due to lobbying by that denomination. In 1943, the government also established a few CPS camps run directly by Selective Service to take some of those designated "troublemakers" off the churches' hands.

Very few sociological or psychological studies have been conducted on those in CPS, and none have been done on pacifists in prison during World War II. Two of the handful conducted on CPS members, unfortunately, have serious methodological flaws.[5] One of the best studies was a sociological analysis of men in Friends camps. The study was conducted by Adrian

E. Gory and David C. McClelland and published in 1947.[6] Gory
and McClelland found that the average camper in the Friends
CPS had attained considerably more education than the average
military conscript, suggesting a predominantly middle-class
C.O. population in Friends camps. They also found that 70 percent of those from Friends CPS scored in the highest stratum
of the military's intelligence test, while only 9 percent of army
inductees scored in that range. These data should be treated
with caution, for intelligence tests can be poorly designed and
applied, but they do suggest a pacifist community of highly in-
telligent, well-educated men in the Friends camps. The experience of being shipped off to do years of unpaid menial labor
was particularly frustrating for these young men.

Although the Selective Training and Service Act stipulated
that the C.O.s be assigned "work of national importance," it
soon became clear that the military was more concerned with
marginalizing C.O.s in menial tasks during the war years than
with utilizing their impressive training and skills. An illustrative
case was the experience of Don DeVault, who was a chemistry
professor at Stanford University when drafted. Sent to a CPS
camp in Mancos, California, DeVault was assigned to dig ditches
and drive trucks. DeVault asked for "detached service" to pursue
potentially important research into penicillin, but, according to
the *Washington Post,* "the sole outcome of the plea was an order
transferring him to the Government camp at Germfask
where rebellious or 'noncooperative' objectors are concentrated." DeVault responded by going on a work strike, for which
he was placed in prison. "If there is any sense in this wasting of
a man's skill," the *Post* editorialized, "we cannot see it. . . . We
say that this [treatment] is stupid and ugly—and unbecoming to
a great free people engaged in a war for the freedom of the
human conscience."[7]

DeVault's was not an isolated case. For the most part, despite
their high educational attainment and oft-repeated desire to do
something more constructive as an alternative to military service, C.O.s were sent to do menial work in remote areas. "In
practice," historian Lillian Schlissel sums up, "CPS proved to be

an extension of the Civilian Conservation Corps started during the depression of the 1930s."[8]

The C.O. prison population also swelled during the war years. The handful who had resisted the peacetime draft were joined by thousands after Pearl Harbor. All told, about six thousand conscientious objectors were imprisoned during the war, constituting approximately one-sixth of all males in federal prisons.[9] Of these, 4,300 were Jehovah's Witnesses with little or no political agenda. They were imprisoned because the government did not recognize the claim that every member of the church was a minister deserving of the draft exemption for clergy. The remaining seventeen hundred, however, constituted the most militant distinct group of pacifists in the nation. Most of this group were in prison because they had refused to register for the draft, either because they did not believe the state had the right to coerce them to do anything or because they felt CPS was a sham, or for both reasons. A few, such as DeVault, made their way to prison via CPS camps, where disenchantment had led them to go on strike or to "walk out" or to otherwise be arrested for being less than happy campers. This prison population coalesced around Dellinger and his fellows who made the prison experience a laboratory for a new, radical pacifism. Early in the war, strikes began to spread beyond the initial Union Eight action at Danbury. By 1943, federal prisons across the country were almost incessantly disrupted by strikes. While Danbury continued to be politically restive, in 1943 Lewisburg Penitentiary in Pennsylvania was vying for the honor of being the most militant prison in the country. Again, Dellinger was at the center of the activity.

The Union Eight, who had been sentenced to a year and a day at Danbury, were released on parole in September of 1941. Because the men still refused to register, the warden at Danbury filled out and signed their registration forms against their wishes. Although they refused to accept their registration certificates, they were given parole for having "complied" with registration.[10]

Dellinger returned to his wife and young son at the Newark

ashram, where in 1943 he organized the People's Peace Now Committee. Calling for an immediate end to the war was a radical stance in 1943, even within pacifist circles, because there was such strong feeling about the Pearl Harbor attack and because so many American lives had already been lost in the war effort. The People's Peace Now Committee managed to engage in very few pickets before its leaders were arrested, many of them charged with Selective Service violations.

When he founded the committee, Dellinger was already appealing a draft board decision that would soon send him back to prison. In October of 1941, a little over a month after being released from Danbury, Dellinger found himself being drafted into the military, his local draft board ostensibly acting upon the bogus registration form signed by the warden at Danbury. Dellinger wrote to his board: "My religious opposition to the whole war system, of which conscription is an obvious part, made it impossible for me to register or cooperate with the Selective Service Act. I have already served a sentence of one year and one day for this. . . . Therefore it will be impossible for me to report for a physical examination." [11]

The draft board's response was unequivocal. Unanimously recommending to the attorney general that Dellinger be prosecuted yet again for violating Selective Service rules, Dellinger's board seized the occasion to pontificate on the proper handling of conscientious objectors:

> Citizenship should be taken from them regardless of their birthplace and, as soon as it is practicable, all such should be removed from the soil they refuse to defend. If they had their choice, either to move to other countries or be placed upon some mandated islands in the Pacific, or quartered on the outposts of our civilization, perhaps they would see the light. . . . Cowards, slackers, and hypocrites, who hide behind so-called conscientious scruples, must be denied membership in a free society. We owe it to our fighting men, and to those citizens who are patriotically working for our preservation, to make an example of those who refuse. They have no place here and this country

must spew them forth as an element inimical to the national welfare.[12]

Given the attitude of his board, it is little wonder that Dellinger found himself in early 1943, at the age of twenty-eight, married, with a young child and another on the way, sentenced to two years at Lewisburg Penitentiary in western Pennsylvania.

When Dellinger arrived at Lewisburg, he heard that Bill Sutherland had just begun a C.O. strike against segregation there. Sutherland, an African-American who credits Dellinger's influence for his decision to become a pacifist while a college student in the 1930s, had been living at the Newark ashram until he was arrested in 1942. A white southern judge sentenced him to four years in the penitentiary, twice as long as any sentence that had been meted out to a C.O. up to that point. Having grown up in a relatively tolerant and affluent biracial community, Sutherland recalls that he had until then "accepted a class analysis" of racism. "Although I had experienced various types of discrimination, being in a privileged position it hadn't hit me at that time." His wartime prison experience would convince Sutherland that racism was a factor independent of class in American society.[13]

The strike at Lewisburg in 1943 began when Sutherland refused to sit at the table designated for blacks in the cafeteria. Some other C.O.s had initially shown their support for Sutherland by willingly taking their trays into the cafeteria but refusing to eat. After a few days, weakened from not eating, they also refused to work. At that point, Sutherland recalls, "we were put in the 'hole,' so to speak. I think there were about 19 of us, altogether, who were put in the hole. Then after we made this protest, we filled up all the holes for the recalcitrants, . . . so we did get integrated in the sense that they put us all—I think there may have been over time two or three of us who were African-American—but they put us all into a dormitory."[14] Dellinger joined the strikers before he had even been fully processed upon his arrival at the prison.

By August of 1943, three months after the strike began, the

C.O.s had broadened their demands to include an end to censorship at the prison. This confluence of demands was typical of militant C.O.s during the war, for they felt that racial injustice was but one aspect of the broader infringement upon the freedom of the individual they posited in modern society. While on strike, Dellinger had also undergone an intense personal experience with mail censorship. "At the time of this strike," he wrote in 1948, "my wife was nearing the end of a difficult pregnancy. The prison authorities knew this, and they also knew that she had been seriously ill in a previous pregnancy, which had ended in a miscarriage. For three weeks they kept all mail from me. Then the acting Warden came into my cell and told me that my wife was dying. She had sent word that I must abandon the strike. . . . Later the prison doctor came in and told me the same thing. It was not until many weeks later that I found out for sure that she had not been ill at all, and had been writing me encouraging letters all the while." [15] This and similar experiences convinced some C.O.s that the strike was broadly against the kind of society that would allow such prisons.

Finally, in part because pacifist groups on the outside such as the Fellowship of Reconciliation and the War Resisters League were publicizing the force-feeding of the prisoners, the director of the Bureau of Prisons, James Bennett, pressured Lewisburg's warden to soften censorship regulations. Although this was far short of the strikers' demands—notably, the prison remained segregated—the exhausted prisoners declared a victory and ended their strike.

By the end of the Lewisburg strike, it was clear that a movement identity was beginning to cohere among the more militant C.O.s, who followed the strikes at Danbury and Lewisburg with much interest from their prisons and even CPS camps across the country. A chain reaction of nonviolent resistance resulted. Danbury prisoners, influenced by the action at Lewisburg, began a second strike of their own against segregation in August of 1943, before the Lewisburg strike ended. Danbury would soon be followed by other prisons and, eventually, some CPS camps. In the process, a new movement, termed by its adherents "radical pacifism," would emerge. According to Bill Sutherland, "[T]here was a sort of underground, and I don't know exactly how it happened, but the thing really just spread—Ashland, Milan, Danbury, all over the place these strikes took place."[16]

In part, news and a sense of shared struggle was conveyed by prisoners who were moved from one facility to another. Also, a network of personal letters and organizational newsletters sprang up. The militants even had their own newsletter, *The Absolutist*, edited by Julius Eichel, who held the distinction of being the only C.O. imprisoned in both world wars. *The Absolutist*, as proclaimed in its masthead, was "devoted to the interests of those with conscientious scruples against any form of war service." A typical passage from *The Absolutist* reveals how effective this informal network was in catalyzing chain reactions throughout the extended C.O. community: "Igal Roodenko and Jack Smock at Mancos, Colo. CPS camp upon hearing of the Lewisburg fast decided on October 12th [1943] to join them in a sympathy fast. Smock continued working, while Roodenko, who quit work, was arrested. . . . In addition, ten COs in the Federal Correctional Institution at Ashland, Ky., are engaged in an eight day hunger strike, ending November 7th, in support of the men at Lewisburg. As far as can be learned one man is still fasting. At Danbury Correctional Institution the men in isolation are beginning to show physical effects of their long isolation."[17]

FOUNDING THE CONGRESS OF RACIAL EQUALITY

Meanwhile, the C.O. strikes against segregation in the prisons helped galvanize the formation of a group of young people committed to direct action against Jim Crow in the larger society. One of their leaders was George Houser, who had been writing his senior thesis under Niebuhr when he joined the Union Eight. Enthused by his participation in the strike at Danbury, Houser wrote to A. J. Muste of the Fellowship of Reconciliation in June of 1941: "It seems to me that the time has definitely arrived for those of us who . . . favor the creation of a society with greater justice for all to create a movement which can take us in that direction. . . . We must raise up a movement based on non-violence as a method, with the immediate aim of opposing the war, of preserving as much democracy as possible here at home, and of working ultimately for a more socialistic society." Houser's enthusiasm was typical of those pacifists radicalized during the war years. Far from feeling despondent about the overwhelming popular support for the war effort in the United States, radical pacifists found the shared resistance and the sense of emerging movement in their distinct camp and prison communities exhilarating. Many felt that in nonviolent direct action, which was proving so effective at disrupting their places of internment, they had found a philosopher's stone capable of revolutionizing the broader society after the war. Houser confidently asserted that "there are literally thousands of young people throughout the country who are just waiting to line up with some such group as this," the radical pacifist program he had outlined.[18]

Released from prison in late 1941, Houser moved to Chicago to complete his seminary training at the University of Chicago. This decision was prompted by two visits he had received while in Danbury. One was from Henry Sloane Coffin of Union, who told Houser he could only return to complete his seminary training at Union if he agreed to clear all his political actions through the school's administration. The other was from A. J. Muste, who offered Houser a job as field secretary for the Fellowship of Reconciliation (FOR) in the Chicago area upon his release from prison.

Due to his experience in the prison strikes against segregation, Houser had become very interested in exploring direct action tactics as the basis for a movement for racial equality. Houser began to meet with a small group of graduate and undergraduate students at the University of Chicago who shared these concerns. Most of them were white, middle-class members of the FOR. The group met every Saturday to study readings on Gandhi and nonviolence; then they would discuss "ways in which the nonviolent method might by adapted to deal with racism here in America."[19] This group had six regular members, of whom, according to historians August Meier and Elliot Rudwick, "all [were] pacifists; three served terms in jail or CPS camp as conscientious objectors. Four were white, two were black."[20] From this small study group would emerge the Congress of Racial Equality (CORE).[21]

In January of 1942, the study group, which then called itself the Chicago Council Against Racial and Religious Discrimination, decided to challenge Chicago's de facto racial districting by renting a group house in an all-white section of the city. The signers of the lease were white, but they were to be joined by blacks upon taking up residence. The hoped-for confrontation with real estate practices did not materialize, because the six-month lease proved too short for such an action, but the plan helped to further focus the group on creative challenges to segregation.

At this time, in January of 1942, James Farmer, who was closely involved in the Chicago group's housing action, sent a memorandum to A. J. Muste for comment. Farmer, a young African-American who had recently graduated from Howard University, was then working as the FOR's race relations secretary. In his letter to Muste, Farmer audaciously called for a national movement of civil disobedience to dismantle segregation in a program he called "Brotherhood Mobilization." Brotherhood Mobilization was in many ways the Chicago study and action group writ large. "I urge," Farmer wrote Muste, "that the Fellowship of Reconciliation . . . immediately lay plans for launching a nation-wide Brotherhood Mobilization," which Farmer wanted "placed on a Five-Year Plan or even a Ten-Year Plan, after which, it is to be hoped, relentless non-cooperation, economic boycott, civil disobedience, etcetera, will be thrown into swing wherever and whenever necessary." In contrast to the liberal Urban League and NAACP, which he dismissed as having "demonstrated their inadequacy in dealing effectively with . . . race in America," Farmer envisioned a "virile" and "comprehensive" program "such as our study and experimentation in non-violence should logically lead into." "Above all,"

Farmer boldly concluded, "the Brotherhood Mobilization must present a distinctive and radical approach. It must strive . . . not to make racial discrimination more bearable, but to wipe it out."[22]

The man to whom Farmer sent his memo, A. J. Muste, was executive secretary for the Fellowship of Reconciliation, the pacifist organization for which Farmer and most members of the Chicago group worked, and the most influential pacifist in the United States. Muste's post at the helm of the FOR, the largest nondenominational pacifist organization in the country, gave him a high profile in pacifist circles and access to institutional resources few other pacifists had. Muste also knew virtually every radical and liberal leader in the country on a first-name basis, for his personal history had spanned the entire activist spectrum on the Left over the previous three decades.[23]

Born in 1885, Muste had had an unremarkable career as a young minister in the Dutch Reformed Church in the early years of the twentieth century. In 1914, however, Muste began to show the first signs of a spiritual restiveness that would send him on an epic quest across the entire landscape of the American Left. Leaving the church he had been raised in because he could no longer abide its fundamentalism, Muste took a pastorship in 1914 at a Congregational church, where he adopted the unpopular position that Christian faith required absolute pacifism. This belief led him in 1915 to organize the first American branch of the Fellowship of Reconciliation, which had been established by British pacifists the previous year. When the United States entered World War I, Muste's congregation forced him out for continuing to preach against war.

While he and his family were being financially supported by a sympathetic group of Quakers, Muste went as an observer to the Wobbly-led (Industrial Workers of the World [IWW]) textile strike at Lawrence, Massachusetts, in 1919. Seeing first-hand the conditions the workers lived and worked in, as well as the brutal police repression of the strikers, Muste threw himself into the union cause, soon becoming head of the strike committee. Muste himself was severely beaten and almost framed with a murder charge by the local police and militia during the strike.

After the strike ended, a much-radicalized Muste secured a position as director of Brookwood Labor College, a post he held. from 1921 to 1933. The idyllic setting of the college on an estate in the countryside north of New York City gave his wife and children a much-needed respite from the turmoil he had dragged them through in following his spiritual and political muse. Although in many ways a compassionate man, Muste, according to his biographer, Joann Ooiman Robinson, had a "persistent habit of placing his principles before the comfort of those directly dependent on him." Muste, Robinson says, "clearly felt that, because he was working for a greater good, the strains and uncertainties to which his work subjected his loved ones were justified."[24]

During this period, Muste identified himself as a Marxist, repudiating his religious and pacifist past. He used the college as a pulpit to denounce what he considered the timidity of the AFL and to advocate industrial unionism (which was commonly referred to as "Musteism" for a time in the 1920s). In 1933, Muste left Brookwood with a contingent of teachers loyal to him to found the American Workers party (AWP), which espoused violent labor confrontation. Within a year, however, Muste was duped into fusing the AWP with the Communist League of America, led from abroad by Leon Trotsky, on terms that resulted in Trotskyist control of Muste's group.

Yet Muste's life was on the verge of another epiphany. In 1936, friends who were concerned about the exhaustion he and his family were showing pooled donations to send them on a European vacation. Muste visited Trotsky in Norway, but they were unable to resolve their differences. While sitting quietly in a medieval church during a sight-seeing tour of Paris, the fifty-one-year-old Muste experienced a powerful reconversion to Christianity, which he also immediately equated with a rededication to pacifism. Applying his usual intensity now again to pacifism, Muste by 1940 once more assumed the leadership of the American FOR, which he had founded in 1915. A 1939 *Time* magazine article on conscientious objection, which referred to him as "the No. 1 U.S. pacifist," quoted Muste as say-

A. J. Muste, October 1958. Photo by David McReynolds, reprinted with permission from the War Resisters League files.

ing, "Go to the front but refuse to kill," a position strikingly similar to the Trotskyist strategy of maintaining outward conformity to the status quo until the appropriate revolutionary movement.[25]

In the year before writing his famous memo, Farmer had worked closely with Muste on segregation issues. In 1941, Muste had dispatched Farmer and Bayard Rustin, another young black FOR organizer, to work with A. Philip Randolph's March on Washington Movement. Randolph, who devoted most of the 1930s to organizing the Brotherhood of Sleeping Car Porters, the first all-black nationwide labor union, had threatened to lead ten thousand blacks in a march against job discrimination in the nation's capital in 1941. Concerned about maintaining tranquility on the domestic labor and racial fronts during the coming war, President Roosevelt quickly issued the landmark Executive Order 8802 in June 1941. This order, which established the Fair Employment Practices Committee and opened the doors to black entry into wartime industry, succeeded in persuading Randolph to call off his march. Randolph, however, maintained his organization as the March on Washington Movement (MOWM), keeping alive the threat of a march to maintain pressure on administration policy.[26]

Muste felt that the MOWM should be encouraged to pursue forms of action other than marches. He and George Houser were also disturbed by the MOWM's exclusion of whites, which Muste felt was antithetical to pacifism and counterproductive, because it made it difficult to gather white liberal support for racial equality. Muste, accordingly, sent the two most prominent blacks on the FOR's payroll, James Farmer and Bayard Rustin, to work with Randolph for much of 1941 and 1942 in an attempt to steer the MOWM in a biracial and tactically broader direction.

Having worked closely with Muste on national race issues, then, Farmer hoped for an affirmation of his bold blueprint for Brotherhood Mobilization when he posted his memo in January of 1942. Farmer recalls that he mailed the memo "airmail special delivery from the post office, not a mailbox, to ensure its speedy arrival to the hands of Muste. I slammed the envelope down on the counter in front of the clerk as if I were, by that act, driving the first nail into the coffin of racism in America."[27] Muste, however, had learned caution by his mid-fifties. With close ties to liberals and some government leaders, Muste was keenly aware of how limited pacifism's potential influence was during the war years. In addition, Muste headed an antiwar organization whose membership consisted mostly of traditional pacifists who espoused moral suasion but shrank from the new emphasis on confrontation espoused by young men such as Farmer and Dellinger. Muste was also aware of what he termed "the Jim Farmer problem"[28]—that Farmer was far more effective at speaking and writing than at following through with the nitty-gritty of organizing. Muste disappointed Farmer with but lukewarm encouragement: "It has given me a much clearer picture of what you have in mind, and it enables me to visualize the possibilities, which I feel are very real." Muste added that he considered "the chance of getting any support from foundations" to be "almost nil" and urged Farmer to "do some more thinking" about his plan.[29] Farmer writes that the first time the two had a chance to meet to discuss Brotherhood Mobilization, Muste, much to Farmer's chagrin, reprimanded him for not being a better organizer.[30]

Muste had a complex relationship with the younger generation of radicals. On the one hand, his stature and access to resources made him someone young fire-eaters such as Farmer and Dellinger wanted to nudge into the radical camp. Muste's own radical background also made him one of the few older pacifist leaders who remained open to the younger militants. Yet Muste had at least temporarily outgrown his most militant phase, and he now had a broader constituency to serve. Often in these years he tried to support all sides at once. Muste, for instance, was almost alone among prominent older pacifists in supporting the Union Eight's decision to refuse their religious exemption.[31] On the other hand, he also gave strong FOR support to the CPS camp experiment, for which Dellinger castigated him as the leader of the "Fellowship of Reconciliation-with-Evil."[32] Similarly, although Muste funded the Congress of Racial Equality with FOR money through its first years, Farmer and some other CORE members eyed him skeptically for his unwillingness to commit himself wholeheartedly to the cutting edge of nonviolent militancy against segregation.

Farmer's ideas for an organization of political cells across the nation engaging in a sustained campaign of civil disobedience against segregation were, however, received enthusiastically by the members of the Chicago study group. A few years later, Houser would write that "the Saturday afternoon group spent many sessions discussing the plan and thought that here was a basis for organizing an interracial nonviolent movement in this country."[33] Farmer's memorandum helped crystalize the thinking of group members and became a catalyst for further action. One outcome of the enthusiasm the memo generated was the appointment of a temporary organizing committee within the Chicago group, led by George Houser and Bernice Fisher, another white FOR member. The committee's charge was to develop a feasible action sensational enough to generate attention and help build a national movement.

The first action organized by the committee was an attempt to desegregate Chicago's White City Roller Rink.[34] This rink was rumored to use a fictitious membership policy to keep blacks out—only blacks were asked to show membership cards, which did not exist. In April 1942, twenty-four activists, many of them students the Chicago group had recruited, arrived in separate groups of blacks and whites to expose this policy. As expected, only the black group was asked to prove membership when requesting admission. After fruitless negotiations with the manager, the Chicago group took the rink to court. Unfortunately, many of the student witnesses had graduated or moved away before the case was tried. Nonetheless, this action, while not the sensational media event that had been hoped for, did generate some publicity within pacifist circles, and it helped to further solidify the Chicago group into a coherent organization. After the White City action, the group established a permanent committee and, in June, adopted the name Congress of Racial Equality (CORE).

The preposition in that name was chosen after considerable thought and discussion. The radical pacifists who founded CORE operated in an American reform tradition that espoused the faith that if a small group of people—or even an individual—behaves in a utopian fashion, the results could be revolutionary for the entire society. This reform tradition stretched back at least to the colonial Quakers and included the Garrisonians and Thoreau, whose example radical pacifists often cited to support their actions. Historically, this utopian reformism has often taken religious forms. Groups such as the Quakers, for instance, have sometimes acted upon the hope that if only a few people act in the present as if the Kingdom of God were already arrived, placing themselves at odds with contemporary mores, the effect would help shatter present social reality to initiate the arrival of that Kingdom. Such beliefs infused much of the Social Gospel movement, as well. The discussions that led the small group forming CORE to carefully select the name Congress *of* Racial Equality instead of Congress *for* Racial Equality stood solidly in this tradition. CORE's founders hoped that if they, the Beloved Community, acted as though the Kingdom of racial justice were already present among them—by going into restaurants and other public facilities as if segregation did not exist—then the tension generated between the higher justice they represented and the injustice of current historical circumstances would be transformative for the entire society.

CORE chose to be organizationally autonomous, but it maintained close ties with the FOR. In fact, throughout the group's first years, the vast majority of its funding came from Muste, including the salaries for many officers such as Houser, and its more active membership continued to be drawn from the FOR. Bernice Fisher was the first CORE chairman—the gender-specific language of that title reflecting the group's notions of male leadership. Fisher was soon moved to the position of secretary-treasurer, the more common position for women in radical organizations at the time. Farmer then became CORE's chairman, while Houser, as executive secretary, oversaw the day-to-day details from his FOR office. Small CORE cells quickly spread to other cities in the following year, in part due to the combination of Farmer's talents as a speaker with Houser's gift for organizing. CORE also benefited from the publicity sparked by its continuing actions.

One of the major actions CORE took in 1942 occurred when Bayard Rustin came to visit Chicago in November. Rustin and Farmer knew each other well from the work they had done together in the March on Washington Movement under Muste's direction. Rustin himself had worked with the Young Communist League in the 1930s before being converted to pacifism by Muste. A man of extraordinary intellectual, organizational, musical, and oratorical talents, Rustin soon wielded significant influence in both the MOWM and the FOR. Rustin became particularly close to Muste, who at times seemed to be a father figure for him. Bill Sutherland, who became a lifelong friend of Rustin's when they met in college, remembers that Rustin and Muste shared a general outlook informed by their Marxist backgrounds: "They tended to do a lot of work together in bringing the conversations [in meetings] to their own [agenda]. We used to joke about it and call them the 'Rusty-Muste Axis.'"[35] Another activist, Dave McReynolds, remembers Rustin as "a kind of evangelical preacher for the gospel of nonviolence" who was "the great existential figure in my life." McReynolds, too, felt that Rustin and Muste complemented each other. Muste, he remembers, had a "genuine Bolshevik commitment . . . which Bayard didn't have." Rustin, on the other hand, was Muste's "hands and feet and eyes," because he was better at organizational planning than Muste, whose sense of urgency sometimes led him to make decisions that were "inept organizationally." (McReynolds recalls Rustin explaining some of Muste's near-sighted allocations of FOR resources as due to the fact that "he wants a revolution before he dies.")[36]

Bill Sutherland recalls that Rustin "loved to be in crisis situations."[37] In fact, Rustin developed a reputation for physical courage. In 1942, for instance, acting entirely on his own and without backup, Rustin refused to take a back seat on a bus going from Louisville to Nashville. After he was manhandled at the Nashville police station, the police captain shouted at him: "Nigger, you're supposed to be scared when you come in here!" Rustin replied, "I am fortified by truth, justice, and Christ. . . . There is no need to fear."[38] John Nevin Sayre of the FOR wrote in 1944 that "all of us in the Fellowship office here . . . admire and love Bayard very much. . . . He has a combination of gifts . . . [that] will take him very far, . . . if he can maintain his inner sweetness and humility of spirit, on the one hand in the face of the bitter sufferings of the Negro race, . . . and on the other against the adulation which will come his way because of his talents and personality."[39]

Upon remarking that he needed a haircut while visiting the Chicago area in 1942, Rustin was told that a barber shop on the University of Chicago campus refused to serve blacks. Rustin soon decided to put it to the test by arriving in the shop shortly before James Robinson, a white CORE member. When the barber went to serve Robinson, he and Rustin both insisted that Rustin be served first. The barber refused, and the ensuing discussion was overheard by a teacher at the Divinity School. A committee subsequently formed of CORE members and Divinity School faculty that successfully negotiated the desegregation of the shop after threatening a boycott.

Such actions encouraged similar ones elsewhere. In January 1943, at the Golden Lantern Restaurant in Denver and the Alhambra Roller Rink in Syracuse, in March of that year at theaters in Denver, and in April at the Greenfield Cafeteria in Detroit, small CORE cells engaged in confrontational actions to challenge de facto segregation in public places. These actions were, at best, only marginally successful, but they encouraged many of the participants to continue to pursue direct action tactics. At CORE's first national conference, held in Chicago in June 1943, a little over a year after the group's founding, delegates reported actions against segregation being taken by CORE groups in seven cities across the country.[40]

The conference committee decided to use the first national

gathering as an opportunity to engage in direct action with a larger group. George Houser was put in charge of planning the action. The target Houser selected was Stoner's, a restaurant in Chicago's loop. In late 1942, a few CORE members had been refused service there. Subsequent investigation found that, despite the owner's insistence that serving blacks would hurt business, Stoner's was the only one of some fifty restaurants in the loop that discriminated. An unsuccessful campaign to change Stoner's policy by meetings, pickets, and boycott throughout early 1943 satisfied Gandhian precepts of trying the least coercive methods first. The time seemed right to take direct action against Stoner's in what the organizers hoped would also double as a rousing culmination of CORE's first national conference.

In all, sixty-five CORE members participated in the Stoner's action, sixteen of them black. Houser decided to use a sit-in tactic similar to the strike method used by the United Automobile Workers against General Motors in Flint, Michigan, in 1937. This method had been used against segregation in some sporadic instances before, but CORE's sit-in at Stoner's was the first well-organized, systematic use of the sit-in tactic against Jim Crow facilities in American history. It was also engaged in by a considerably larger group than in any similar action up to that time.

One of the challenges facing the protesters was that the restaurant sat over two hundred people, too large to easily disrupt. This was one reason it seemed best to attempt the Stoner's action when the numbers of the Chicago CORE were swelled by conference attenders. Houser decided to place protesters in different places around the large restaurant. White participants would arrive first in small groups to be dispersed at different tables. Later, two interracial groups would arrive to request seating. All participants were asked to commit to remaining seated all night, if necessary, until the two interracial groups were served.

On the evening of the protest, the all-white groups were able to fan out to tables around the restaurant without difficulty, as anticipated. When the first interracial group arrived, the management ignored them while seating white customers who arrived later. After a tense half-hour, to protesters' surprise, the interracial group was seated, although Mr. Stoner kicked one of them in the shins on the way to the table. The seating of the first interracial group was the cue for the second to arrive. This was too much for Stoner. Business came to a halt and, during the next hour-and-a-half, he called the police in three times. The police, however, refused to make any arrests, since the protesters were breaking no law, but they did threaten to arrest Mr. Stoner if he called them again. Finally, the deadlock in the restaurant was broken when an elderly white woman not affiliated with CORE invited a black member of the second group to sit at her table. The all-white CORE groups that had been seated quickly did the same. At this, most of the customers erupted in spontaneous applause—support that particularly moved the protesters. Stoner's was desegregated and would remain so in subsequent years.

Most of these early CORE actions were tame by the standards of subsequent black freedom struggles. They took place outside the South where the law and significant segments of public opinion were supportive of challenges to segregation. Yet these early successes, while not reaching into the deep South, did galvanize CORE protesters into a cohesive national organization committed to exploring the cutting edge of nonviolent militancy against racial discrimination. The delegates from CORE's first national convention, certainly, went home with a heady sense of success. The systematic campaign culminating in a disciplined sit-in at Stoner's constituted a germinal contribution made by these radical pacifists to the nonviolent arsenal of the future Civil Rights Movement and of social protest in general. There would be other, equally significant, contributions radical pacifists in CORE would make to desegregation protest in subsequent years.

About the time of the Stoner action, the efforts of Muste, Farmer, and Rustin to steer the most influential civil rights leader in the country in new directions seemed to be paying off. In early 1943, A. Philip Randolph threw his support behind a nationwide campaign of civil disobedience against segregation that had been urged upon him by Muste and his two FOR staff members. At the annual convention of the March on Washington Movement (MOWM) in July of that year, delegates endorsed the plan, which called for designating one day each week for blacks across the nation to refuse to follow segregated arrangements.

The FOR influence on this new direction was evident from the prominence of its members at the MOWM convention. Jay Holmes Smith, an FOR member at the convention, wrote eagerly to Muste that "the historic decision to adopt NVDA [nonviolent direct action] as a major method and strategy of the MOWM was unanimously made. . . . Rusty [Rustin] spoke most effectively on it, climaxing with a deep and searching note, asking us to bow our heads and breaking out with 'It's Me, O Lord, Standin' in the Need of Prayer.'" Rustin, by all accounts, could have chosen a career as a professional singer. Smith notes in the same letter that "Rusty's message was an excellent preparation for the next morning's program, entirely devoted to NVDA," at which James Farmer spoke about techniques.[41] Muste was thrilled. Earlier in the year, when Randolph first announced that he would attempt to get the MOWM to endorse such CORE-like tactics, Muste wrote to extend his "personal word of congratulation at the vision, intelligence and courage represented by this step. . . . This action of yours may well prove as epoch-making as Gandhi's own inauguration of a similar movement in South Africa in 1906."[42]

Faced with considerable opposition, however, the proposed campaign never materialized. Randolph withdrew his support from the plan. Some historians have suggested a skittish black press and mainstream white reaction to recent race riots in Detroit as major factors in that decision.[43] Such a plan, at any rate, was no doubt overly ambitious, too broad to easily organize and vulnerable to brutal repression.

Randolph's plan also lacked liberal support among both whites and blacks in the war years. In response to Randolph's public support for a campaign of civil disobedience, Muste asked many prominent liberal thinkers (and some radical pacifists) to contribute to a pamphlet addressing the question, "Civil Disobedience: Is It the Answer to Jim Crow?" Only a few respondents, including Bernice Fisher and Muste himself, supported Randolph. Most opposed his plan, among them Reinhold Niebuhr, Roger Baldwin, and Norman Thomas.[44]

This lack of liberal support revealed how radical civil disobedience was perceived to be in the early 1940s. Randolph's quick retreat from adopting this militant strategy meant that nonviolent direct action against segregation would remain the tactic of choice for only a small band of radical pacifists centered around CORE for more than a decade to come. This was also not the last time Randolph would abruptly call off a direct action campaign urged upon him by radicals associated with the FOR: a similar course of events would take place when Muste and Randolph temporarily joined forces to resist the draft and segregation in the armed forces in the late 1940s. Each time, the distrust between the Muste and Randolph forces increased, Randolph feeling manipulated by the radical pacifists and Muste feeling betrayed by a perceived lack of follow-through on Randolph's part.

C.O. STRIKES

Meanwhile, strikes against segregation continued in the prisons throughout 1943. Imprisoned C.O.s and CORE members, many themselves recently released from the penitentiary, kept close tabs on the ongoing radical resistance to racism both outside and inside the prisons. Inspiration went in both directions. Prison strikes during the war yielded some of CORE's most important recruits, including the young fire-eater, Jim Peck. Bayard Rustin, on the other hand, did not go to prison as a C.O. until 1944. Once at the penitentiary in Ashland, Kentucky, Rustin wasted no time in refusing to eat at a segregated table, initiating one of the largest prison strikes of the war period.

Imprisoned pacifists continued to protest about a variety of issues, but strikes increasingly focused on segregation. This was a natural issue for C.O.s, many of whom were raised in the Social Gospel tradition and many of whom, as northerners, were experiencing their first direct encounter with enforced segregation while in prison. There was also an instrumental reason for this focus: imprisoned C.O.s found that protests against segregation received more response from traditional pacifist organizations and the general public than did similar protests against the war. Even the prison system showed more responsiveness when the issue was race, in part because this was a vulnerable spot for the national government at a time when the Roosevelt administration was struggling to ensure black support for the war effort. It was also potentially embarrassing to war propaganda that portrayed the United States as the defender of liberty for the country to be plagued by racial conflict at home.[45]

One of the radical pacifists' strengths during this period was their very experimentalism, which allowed them to respond flexibly to changing conditions. Radical pacifist groups were the first white-led groups on the American Left to shift their agenda away from labor, which continued to be a fetish of the Old Left, toward a focus on race and militarism. James Farmer wrote to Muste as early as 1942: "There are two great fields in which our contemplations have rested, the industrial and the racial. For obvious reasons, the former has been temporarily cancelled as a field for great activity along these [direct action] lines. But the latter remains, probably more urgent today than ever before since slavery."[46] Houser wrote along similar lines in the early 1940s: "A mass movement is needed. . . . The masses of Negroes are ready and waiting for it. They are increasingly restless under petty discriminations which confront them constantly. They are going to take action against this petty discrimination. Therefore it is important that this action be organized group action. . . , rather than simply being dissipated in individual action."[47] The focus on race and militarism by radical pacifists in the early 1940s would have important implications for the postwar social activist agenda. As historian Penina M. Glazer has concluded in her study of journals of the Left in the 1940s, "[T]hose groups which were able to rid themselves of total dependence on issues and organizations pertinent in the pre-war period were precisely those to exert considerable influence on the next generation of radical critics. The radical pacifists were particularly dynamic during and after World War II."[48]

Waves of strikes kept the federal penitentiaries in a state of continuous disruption by the end of the war. At Danbury, the first strike to successfully desegregate a federal prison began in August of 1943. One of its organizers was Jim Peck, who wrote a ditty linking American and Nazi racism: "They say that Hitler is wicked / To persecute race in his way / But when it's done in the U.S. / It's quite perfectly OK."[49]

Like many radical pacifists, Peck came from an affluent background. His father was half-owner of the posh women's clothing store, Peck and Peck. Peck's childhood, however, was emotionally deprived: his father was a distant figure and his mother, he later wrote, "seemed devoid of simple humanity." As he began to assert his political radicalism, Peck found himself even further alienated from his mother, who "never ceased ridiculing" his views.[50] When his parents were out, Peck held political meetings in his family's Park Avenue home, to the amusement of his radical friends. Peck's convictions, however, ran deeper than simply a momentary rebellion against his parents' social sensibilities. Peck made major contributions to postwar social activism, participating in nearly every major radical pacifist action from the 1940s to the 1960s. He especially devoted himself to CORE, editing its newsletter from 1949 until the mid-1960s, and he gave large sums of his inheritance to the War Resisters League. Bill Sutherland recalls that Peck had an "IWW personality," showing little tolerance for meetings but enthusiastically participating in dramatic actions. Peck also seemed drawn to "put his body on the line" even more than most of his fellow activists. In fact, he earned a reputation in radical pacifist circles as a valuable man to have at a protest but something of a masochist for his proclivity toward getting beaten during actions.[51]

The Danbury strike lasted for 135 days before the warden capitulated, making Danbury the first federal prison with deseg-

Jim Peck, October 17, 1976. Photo © WRL by Dorothy Marder files.

regated dining facilities. Peck and the other C.O.s were ecstatic over this victory, which they felt had taught them valuable lessons applicable to protest outside the prison walls. "We discovered," Peck later wrote, "that a small number of c.o.'s—totaling not more than 30—could get national and even international publicity for pacifism by means of well-timed public demonstrations of such an unusual nature that the press could not ignore them."[52]

Danbury's success lent renewed vigor to strikes elsewhere—one again in Lewisburg, others at penitentiaries in Petersburg, Milan, and Ashland. At Danbury, too, five absolutists began a strike against the prison system in general on the very day that the strike against segregation ended. While most strikes were against segregation, issues continued to range broadly, leading the federal prisons director James Bennett to marvel at the C.O.s' "uncanny ingenuity at thinking up new issues to raise." One prison superintendent remarked in exasperation: "You c.o.'s may be glad when the war is over but not half as much as I who yearn for the good old days of simple murderers and bank robbers for prisoners!"[53]

IDEOLOGY

One thread of continuity to all the strikes was an expressed desire to disrupt the smooth operation of the prison system by the conscientious resistance of intrepid individuals. Radical pacifists felt that the prison system was the ideal laboratory for experimenting with libertarian resistance, because they believed the United States was rapidly progressing toward totalitarianism. One article in *The Absolutist* neatly summed up this perspective in its title, "America Becoming a Vast Prison Camp."[54]

Much has been written in recent historiography on the "incorporation of America" throughout the late nineteenth and early twentieth century into a more efficiently organized social order—efficient, at any rate, from the perspective of motivating commodity consumption and mobilizing for war.[55] The American government, in waging total war during World War II, utilized, in a far more efficient way than had been the case during World War I, all of the modern resources of propaganda, industrial reorientation, and labor control at the state's command, gearing the entire society to the single purpose of winning the war. Radical pacifists, coming as they were from a strong individualist perspective and highly sensitive to anything that smacked of nascent totalitarianism, believed that a new level of social control was inherent in these developments.

For those who forged the radical pacifist movement, the inviolable constitutive unit of society was the individual. A typical element of preambles to radical pacifist manifestoes was a statement such as that the "growth and integration of the individual personality should be the primary function of society."[56] In this sense, theirs was a thoroughly American radicalism, for it owed a great deal to the American liberal tradition and the individualist mythology that infused American culture. This individualism led the radical pacifists to eschew any official authority. Lewis K. Hill, for instance, wrote in 1947 that the "libertarian revolution" they sought required "a widespread urge to refuse authority and act on a set of principles which might be described as individualist" in order to ensure "the restitution of the individual in a libertarian socialist society."[57] Even the very concept of leadership was suspect. Dave Dellinger, for instance, lamented that "pacifist and socialist agencies have a habit of working for equality by exalting a 'leader' or 'leaders' above the rank and file."[58] The emphasis, instead, was on a rather mystical commitment to total democracy, usually interpreted as consensus decision making by decentralized, local groups. This created dilemmas for those such as Dellinger who naturally assumed leadership roles as a result of their charisma. He and others with leadership qualities had to develop styles of persuasion that adapted their abilities to these unique group dynamics, in which any individual in the group could veto an action and the general ethos of the group was geared toward nonhierarchical decentralism.

Given their commitment to the individual and to unmediated democracy, radical pacifists interpreted the rise of fascism as but a natural extension of the increasing intrusion of corporate structures—industrial as well as governmental—into the lives of people to regiment the work force and nation more effectively. The truly radical response, according to the analysis some C.O.s came to adopt in CPS and prison, was for the individual to make a dramatic symbolic act of resistance. Such resistance, what Muste called "holy disobedience," was designed to challenge assumptions and impede the smooth workings of what were perceived to be unjust institutions in the larger society. Such action also was intended to reassert the autonomy of the individual in corporate society—a society, radical pacifists were convinced, on the same evolutionary path as fascist Europe. To these C.O.s, the spontaneous chain reaction among militant pacifists interned during the war proved the creativity and motley but intrepid solidarity of which uncompromising individualists were capable. This gave them hope that their acts of resistance during the war were paradigms for the revolutionary reassertion of individual freedom throughout society.

From this perspective, radical pacifists felt theirs was the only true protest against the increasing regimentation and authoritarianism they posited in the mass society. Traditional pacifism, as evidenced by its role in CPS, was dismissed as complicit with the government by these Young Turks. Marxism, with its emphasis on hierarchy, centralism, and collective discipline, was seen as merely another version of the authoritarianism they opposed in the U.S. government. Radical pacifists throughout the 1940s and 1950s maintained harsh condemnation of the Soviet Union on these grounds.

Dwight Macdonald, editor of the magazine *Politics,* became an influential disseminator and clarifier of these impulses motivating the C.O. activists. Intrigued by the resistance among C.O.s, Macdonald joined the new radical pacifist movement near the end of the war. In 1944, Macdonald articulated what he felt was the significance of their libertarian resistance: "In a period like the present in this country, when there is no immediate prospect of effective political action to realize ultimate principles, there is something very attractive about the c.o.'s kind of individual moral stand. His day-to-day actions and his long-range convictions, if they do not wholly coincide, are at least on speaking terms with each other. . . . The c.o., like the European anarchist or our own old-time Wobblies, at least reacts spontaneously, immediately against the evils he fights, and shapes his everyday behavior to fit his principles. This is a great thing." [59]

There were certainly ideological limits to simply asserting

the individual as a "government-free zone," refusing to cooperate with an American system seen as protototalitarian. There is a certain poverty of analysis in such a stance, not least because the United States was not, in fact, on the verge of becoming fascist. Yet radical pacifists did touch in a distinctively American way upon a concern about the loss of individual autonomy to an increasingly collectivized modern society, a concern that would be shared by growing numbers of people in the following decades.

The person to bring this individualist ethos to its furthest extreme during the war years was Corbett Bishop. Bishop was a former air corpsman with a degree in chemical engineering who, at the beginning of the war, owned a bookstore in New York. He became a pacifist after joining the Church of Christ (a denomination with 198 other men in CPS)[60] and entered a Friends CPS camp in 1942 at the age of thirty-six. Bishop was already disgruntled when he entered the camp, because his induction notice gave him insufficient time to sell his bookstore. He also felt that work without pay was exploitative, an issue that would make many in CPS restive as the war dragged on.

When he was unable to obtain a furlough to settle his business affairs, Bishop went on a forty-four-day hunger strike, during which he lost more than forty-four pounds. After this fast, Bishop began to develop close ties with the FOR group at his camp, which raised money to help him with his bookstore. According to an FOR memo written about his case, Bishop began to deliver a caustic "word-for-the-day" at mealtimes, in which he "did not spare the Historic Peace Churches for their part in administering what he termed 'slavery.'"[61] During 1943, Bishop engaged in two more hunger strikes, one in tandem with Gandhi's twenty-one-day hunger strike for Indian freedom. At the request of the Quaker administration at the camp, he was then removed to the new government-run camp for recalcitrants at Germfask, Michigan. There, Bishop adopted the practice of wearing a ball and chain to symbolize his sense of oppression within CPS.

Finally, when he refused to return to Germfask after a short furlough in 1944, Bishop was arrested. In prison, according to the FOR memo, "he began a policy of complete non-cooperation, insisting that if the state laid hands upon his body, it must take total responsibility for it." During his entire time in prison, he maintained the extreme position of refusing "to eat, move, or even leave his cot to attend to bodily functions."[62] Bishop fasted for eighty-six days while awaiting trial, and then he fasted another 144 days until released on parole. All that while he was force-fed. Because he refused to cooperate with the terms of his parole, Bishop was arrested again and fasted yet another 193 days.[63] During this time, he expressed his stance on CPS to a visitor in these terms: "It never has seemed right and it cannot be right that Christians should be administering a program of conscription for the state where men work . . . at insignificant jobs without pay and without support for their dependents—all as a part of the national program of waging war."[64]

oppose the co cannes

When Bishop's survival came into doubt, he was released on parole despite his refusal to sign release papers. The warden of his prison and a physician drove him from the penitentiary at Milan, Michigan, to Clarksville, Georgia, where Bishop was to recuperate at the Macedonia Cooperative Community. Bishop refused to move himself until he was dropped off at the community.

Release

Once out of the car, Bishop asked the warden, "Is the body free now?" Assured that this was the case, Bishop then stripped naked and placed his government-issued clothes back in the warden's car. A member of the Macedonia community came out with a coat to cover Bishop.[65]

Radical pacifists in the camps and prisons lionized Bishop for forcing state authorities to implicitly acknowledge their inability to control him. Bishop's extreme, almost masochistic, passivity did not arise from a well-formulated political agenda, but his assertion of personal autonomy from any form of coercion made him an icon of sorts in C.O. circles. His story also resonated with many who were similarly radicalized by their disenchantment with CPS.

THE WAR'S END

Toward the end of the war, increasingly radical groups within CPS camps began to emulate the prison strikes. The government-run camp for the most unruly CPS men at Germfask, as might be expected, was the site of the most disruption. There, resistance took a particularly creative turn. Inmates dug ditches with spoons instead of shovels, had to have every ax blow individually ordered when chopping down a tree, pretended to have trouble driving staples into fencing, and became "sick" in alphabetical order.[66]

These forms of resistance, while prankish, are remarkably similar to the resistance Herbert G. Gutman and other historians have chronicled on the part of chattel slaves, with whom the militants in CPS regularly compared their lot.[67] Like the slaves of a century before, C.O.s felt that their labor was being forced from them in uncompensated exploitation, yet most were wary of pushing their resistance too far. Those who were willing to go to prison, such as Bishop and others who "walked out" of CPS, could be more direct in their refusal to cooperate. More than two hundred men in CPS would choose such a course. Radicals who did not want to go to prison, however, had to skirt the edge between resistance and cooperation, as did most slaves in the antebellum South.

The Germfask C.O.s regularly produced a newsletter, which sometimes ran under the heading: "Published from the forced-labor camp operated by the Government of the United States . . . , where conscientious objectors are conscripted to work without pay, provision for dependents, or accident compensation." This newsletter chronicled a taut drama of inmate resistance interchanged with administration intimidation, including the abuse of psychiatric treatment.[68] The newsletter for January 1946 announced that the Germfask camp had finally become completely ungovernable. Germfask, it explained, "was completely 'snafu' last month as practically all camp functioning ceased. Not only was project work of any kind at a standstill, but most camp overhead jobs also went unperformed. . . . After several months of developing breakdown, by Dec. 20 the situation appeared so hopeless to staff members that no project bell was rung again until the 14th of January."[69]

It is no coincidence that Germfask's resistance crested after the end of the war. Men who had worked for years without pay found themselves waiting for months after the surrender of Japan to be released. Adding to their frustration was the fact that the government released C.O.s at slower rates than it demobilized soldiers. As of May 1946 only 44 percent of those in CPS had been discharged.[70] Some C.O.s in prison were not paroled until 1948. Under these circumstances, even the most cooperative assignees grew restive after the cessation of military hostilities. One superintendent of a state mental hospital that had utilized the labor of relatively cooperative men from a Brethren camp, for instance, wrote that he "noted a considerable letdown in the quality of the work following VJ-day."[71] The more militant camps went critical.

The *Germfask Newsletter* of May 1946 opened with the exultant headline, "CPS Strikes across the Nation." One of the most prominent of these postwar strikes was at the Big Flats camp in New York. The *Germfask Newsletter* noted that "Big Flatters believe such action is necessary to direct pacifist efforts against the whole principle of conscription and toward the repudiation of CPS as a dangerous precedent."[72] As was true at many camps, some Big Flatters who had entered CPS in good faith had come to adopt the same critique of CPS as that enunciated by the prison absolutists. Such radicals never constituted a majority within CPS, but they increasingly provided leadership to the majority of campers who were disgruntled that they were being held after the end of the war. Still, there was tension between radical strike leaders and the average striker in CPS. This was evident in a newsletter produced at Big Flats in 1946, which reported considerable disagreement between the majority of strikers, who wanted to pursue quiet negotiations with camp authorities, and the strike organizers, who wanted to engage in more dramatic confrontation. "The dilemma," according to the Big Flats newsletter, "is whether CPS men and pacifists in general should maintain a discreet silence or run the risk of adverse publicity and certain notoriety by speaking out, as well as engaging in 'direct action' projects." The radicals who produced the newsletter complained, "We haven't presented ourselves as even a significant, much less threatening, anti-war threat," for which they blamed "CPS and traditional Peace Church pacifism."[73]

While they never comprised a majority within CPS, then, a critical mass of CPS "campers" did come to identify themselves with the radical pacifist movement that had coalesced around the prison absolutists during the war. The prison and CPS radicals maintained regular, if often indirect, contact, eagerly exchanging ideas and news of actions. Each group gave the other a sense of shared discovery and "movement." The CPS and prison radicals would join forces in the aftermath of the war to create small organizations with a clear sense of identity as rebels with a unique philosophy and agenda.

In 1945, eight CPS veterans wrote to Dave Dellinger and a number of other prison absolutists of their conviction that "the experiences of CPS and prison have revealed and helped to develop elements of a philosophy of radical pacifism which at certain crucial points diverges from the traditional pacifism." Those who recognized "the broad revolutionary implications of pacifism" now "repudiated the philosophy of any pacifist compromise with the conscripting state, supported every phase of civil liberties and racial equality, and sought to develop practical methods of nonviolent action and resistance." The letter writers went on to claim, in true radical pacifist fashion, that "the real war of our age" was one "between individual freedoms and the totalitarian state," and, in this war, "the weapons of nonviolence" were the "unique contribution" of the new radical pacifist movement.[74] Emerging from their wartime incarceration, radical pacifists felt ready to revolutionize postwar America.

Three

REBELS WITHOUT A REVOLUTION,

1945–1952

POSTWAR EXPECTATIONS

On the morning of August 6, 1945, a single bomb exploded above Japan, obliterating tens of thousands of civilians and leaving a razed, irradiated plain where a bustling city had stood moments before. The almost mythic scale of the forces unleashed upon Hiroshima gave most people at least momentary pause. "In 1945," writes Richard Pells in his history of American intellectuals, "the words would not come; the full implications of the atomic bomb could not be grasped." Yet not all were left speechless. "It remained again," Pells notes, "for Dwight Macdonald, writing in *Politics*, to address the issue squarely."[1] Macdonald had an analysis ready to hand because he did not have to struggle to reconcile the way the war ended with his preconceived notions of the way the war had been conducted. Macdonald and other radical pacifists who had long argued that totalitarian tendencies underlay the United States war effort immediately interpreted America's use of the atomic bomb as the culmination and final proof of their analysis. Many radical pacifists in 1945 also confidently assumed that masses of Americans would come to share this analysis once the initial shock waves of the blast began to dissipate.

"This atrocious action," wrote Macdonald in the August 1945 issue of *Politics,* "places 'us,' the defenders of civilization, on a moral level with 'them,' the beasts of Maidanek." Macdonald then went on to list in bold print five conclusions he derived from the bombing of Hiroshima: (1) "[t]he concepts, 'war' and 'progress,' are now obsolete"; (2) "[t]he futility of modern warfare should now be clear," (3) "[a]tomic bombs are the natural product of the kind of society we have created," (4) "[t]hose who wield such destructive power are outcasts from humanity," and (5) "[w]e must 'get' the modern national state before it 'gets' us." Macdonald's concluding advice was that "every individual who wants to save his humanity—and indeed his skin—had better begin thinking 'dangerous thoughts' about sabotage, resistance, rebellion, and the fraternity of all men everywhere."[2]

Dellinger echoed these sentiments in a "Declaration of War" he wrote for the first issue of *Direct Action* magazine, which he began publishing in the autumn of 1945. "The atom bombing of Hiroshima and Nagasaki destroyed whatever claims the United States may have had to being either a 'democratic' or a 'peace-loving' nation," Dellinger proclaimed. "The prejudices of patriotism, the pressures of our friends, and the fear of unpopularity, imprisonment, or death should not hold us back any longer," he added. "Henceforth no decent citizen owes one scrap of allegiance (if he ever did) to American law, American custom, or American institutions. . . . This is total war." The "total war" Dellinger was calling for, of course, was to be a nonviolent struggle. Its totality lay in the comprehensive lifestyle commitment he expected from activists to combat a society that, Dellinger believed, twisted individual personality. "This is a diseased world in which it is impossible for anyone to be fully human," Dellinger asserted. "One way or another, everyone who lives in the modern world is sick or maladjusted." Therefore, Dellinger felt that a person's every action should be a revolutionary assertion: "The acts we perform must be the responsible acts of free men, not the irresponsible acts of conscripts under orders. . . . Every act we perform today must reflect the kind of human relationships we are fighting to establish tomorrow."[3]

Dellinger founded *Direct Action* with other C.O.s almost immediately upon his release from Lewisburg. Throughout late 1945 and early 1946, as evident in the pages of *Direct Action,* radical pacifists exuded confidence that a deep-set revisionism of—indeed, revulsion toward—the Second World War would take hold of the American psyche in the aftermath of the atomic bombing.

Alongside Dellinger's "Declaration of War" in the first issue of *Direct Action* was a "Call to a Conference" drafted by Lew Hill. Like so many radical pacifists, Hill had been reared in affluence. His father was a self-made millionaire who married into the Phillips Petroleum fortune. Hill was a precocious student who enrolled in a special program at Stanford University that allowed him to begin working toward a doctorate immediately after high school. Because the war interrupted his studies, however, Hill never received even an undergraduate degree. While at Stanford, Hill had become enthralled with the work of Gandhi and with the Quaker tradition. When he was drafted, therefore, he registered as a C.O. and was placed in the Coleville, California, CPS camp. Radicalized by his CPS experience, Hill drifted East after the war to join the radical pacifist circle led by Dellinger. Hill soon gained a reputation as an incisive and sometimes caustic intellectual. He was known also for often speaking in cryptic terms. One C.O. recalls being asked by Bayard Rustin: "Hey, do you happen to know Lew Hill? . . . They say that you can't understand what he's talking about."[4]

Hill's announcement in *Direct Action* led to a conference held in Chicago in January 1946. The conference organizers operated on the belief that they were on the verge of a revolutionary situation that would be fueled by a widespread disenchantment with the war. "Instead of capturing political power, we must do away with it," Dellinger boldly declared at a steering

committee meeting held in New York to prepare for the conference. Lew Hill proclaimed simply, "The modern state is the
first enemy. . . . The will to participate must contain the will
to disobey." Looking toward the "revolutionary government"
radical pacifists expected to establish throughout the land, Hill
prescribed that it "must install civil liberties . . . as the supreme
principle." Roy Kepler, a Colorado native who had been removed from no less than six CPS camps before ending up at
Germfask, also attended the New York meeting. As westerners
among East Coast radicals, Hill and Kepler quickly became
friends in 1945. Kepler encouraged the conference organizers
to take out FM radio licenses in order to spread radical pacifist
ideas. This was a pet idea of Hill's, who had been intrigued by
radio since childhood.[5]

The conference drew over one hundred radical pacifists
recently released from camps and prisons across the country.
Proceeding on the assumption that they would soon be restruc-
turing American society along extreme libertarian lines, participants spent much of their time hammering out a sweeping blueprint for the postrevolutionary society, replete with clauses
addressing social equality, the role of cooperatives, and agricul-
tural policy.[6] The conference participants then organized themselves permanently as the Committee for Non-Violent Revolution (CNVR).

While it is easy with historical hindsight to see the efforts
of radical pacifists in the immediate aftermath of World War II
as quixotic, there was some basis for their exaggerated expectations. After all, a strong antiwar reaction had taken hold in the
United States after World War I, even though the war had enjoyed popular support while American soldiers were still in battle. The dismal results of Versailles, the alienation expressed by
ex-patriots such as Hemingway, and investigations into corrup-
tion in the munitions industry by Senator Nye all contributed
to a widespread disillusionment with American participation in
World War I that set in during the 1920s. Radical pacifists hoped
that the use of saturation bombing, and especially the atomic
bombing of Japanese cities, would lead to an even greater revi-

sionism after all became quiet on the fronts of the Second World War. And radical pacifists felt that they could offer disenchanted masses a genuine revolutionary alternative in the methods and program they had developed during the war. The popular reaction they awaited, however, did not come.

In the 1930s, most Americans considered aerial bombardment of civilian populations an atrocity. Its use by fascist forces in Spain in 1936 (which Picasso protested in his painting *Guernica*) and by the Japanese military in China in 1937 were decried in newspapers and pulpits across the United States as barbarous acts unfit for a civilized people. In 1938, the United States senate passed a resolution condemning the bombing of civilian populations as "inhuman." Yet, due to a desire for revenge against the Axis powers and a gradual inurement to the media's images of wartime carnage, the vast majority of Americans supported their own nation's strategic bombing campaigns after Pearl Harbor.[7] American sentiment did not shift back to a repugnance toward bombing civilians after the use of atomic weapons. Quite the contrary. Two days after the detonation over Hiroshima, 85 percent of Americans surveyed approved of the bomb's use. Four months later, 22.7 percent agreed with the statement that "we should have quickly used many more of them before Japan had a chance to surrender."[8] "Ironically," writes historian Neil Katz, "at the same time that pacifism was undergoing a revival, most Americans were converted to the belief that their security rested upon superior, intimidating, military power. . . . Thus the experience of World War II unified the radical pacifists from within but isolated them even more from the mainstream of American society."[9] Radical pacifists would sink precipitately into deeper isolation with the onset of the Cold War in the late 1940s.

By 1947, radical pacifists had begun to let the reality of the historical moment sink in. Lew Hill quickly recognized that no revolutionary momentum existed in the public realm. In the absence of such broad support, Hill criticized CNVR's leadership for continuing to show more interest in protests (which he dismissed as mere exercises in catharsis) than in the nitty-gritty work of modest but constructive projects. In 1948, he described what he perceived to be CNVR's "elementary flaw" to Roy Kepler: "In short, the call for action in the absence of a definite idea is really a call for the individual (particularly the calling individual himself) to express his anxiety (give it release)."[10] Hill chose to detach himself from CNVR to pursue his dream of a radical FM radio station in San Francisco. At a CNVR reevaluation session held in August 1947, he sized up CNVR's situation with his usual pith: "There is no ground yet for a non-violent revolutionary organization. The development of such a group must involve certain key intellectuals around the country very deeply; and it is self-evident that these people have no interest in your battle."[11]

Those who remained committed to CNVR had to reorient their emphases and expectations as it became clear that Americans would be conservative in the postwar period. For peace activists, the late 1940s and 1950s proved lonely years of moving forward with vision while often fighting despair. As hopes for leading a mass movement quickly receded, radical pacifists increasingly fell back upon small group actions and a focus on individual lifestyle choices. CNVR's 1947 conference revealed a dramatic shift toward viewing the political as personal, in marked contrast to the broad manifestoes passionately debated at the 1945 conference. CNVR's *Bulletin* noted that conference participants in 1947 "moved away from the Marxist attitude of dealing with large masses of people, which was felt to be unrealistic in the world today, and toward the concept of working in terms of total life patterns with a few people." One participant commented that "every time someone stops going to the movies it is a gain for the revolution."[12] As the postwar period progressed, radical pacifists came to fancy themselves latter-day Jeremiahs, engaging in small group actions while endlessly obsessing about their personal moral hygiene—an orientation that held a certain allure for these individualists with a taste for moral absolutism. When asked why he refused to pay taxes while conducting a one-man picket at his local IRS office, radical pacifist Ammon Hennacy responded in 1950: "The question is not 'Can

we change the world?' but 'Can we keep the world from changing us?'"[13]

CORE

While this increased focus on individual and small-group lifestyle emerged from tendencies already present in radical pacifist
culture, lifestyle was only given such priority because opportunities for political action on a larger scale were so severely cur-
tailed as the United States entered the Cold War. Yet radical
pacifists still hoped to revolutionize American society, and, so,
they did not become entirely quiescent in this period. They did,
of necessity, gear their activism toward symbolic confrontations
carefully tailored to allow a small number of activists to maximize media coverage. Such symbolic confrontation would become a distinguishing feature of radical pacifism for decades to
come.

Some of the most innovative activism again came from
CORE in the late 1940s. Muste continued to sustain CORE
with FOR money and organizational support throughout the
decade. George Houser, who worked for both organizations,
worried that this arrangement kept CORE in a "dependency
relationship."[14] Muste, on the other hand, felt that the more
moderate pacifism of the FOR was a healthy influence on
CORE. Recalling the excesses of his youthful labor organizing,
Muste wrote Houser in 1944 that "I see no place for an
N.V.D.A. [non-violent direct action] movement to grow effectively and to be healthy, except within the general religious pacifist movement. . . . Such an N.V.D.A. movement operating by
itself would go off the deep end on the use of violence, as a
number of us did after the last war under the stress of first-hand
contact with industrial conflict."[15] All agreed, at any rate, that
the fledgling CORE could not yet financially afford to leave the
FOR nest.

In the mid-1940s, CORE cells continued to spread to cities
around the country. George Houser and Bayard Rustin or-

ganized a series of "interracial workshops" where members learned rudimentary pacifist theory and were taught that "CORE has one method—interracial, direct non-violent action." [16] Role-playing was used to train workshop participants in the use of CORE's "one method," although Houser and Rustin often managed to give attendees a taste of the real thing. At a conference in Toledo in the mid-1940s, for instance, Rustin and Houser were refused service when they went into a local restaurant for lunch. They decided to run the afternoon workshop as a biracial sit-in at the restaurant. After a crowd had gathered outside and the restaurant manager had unsuccessfully attempted to get the police to arrest the protesters, Rustin and Houser were served. Houser recalls that he and Rustin frequently used such spontaneous actions as pedagogy. [17]

While in certain respects CORE was maturing organizationally, Houser, however, feared that the organization was failing to develop a national identity and agenda, that it was little more than "a loose federation of local groups . . . united mostly by their aim of tackling discrimination by a particular method—nonviolent direct action." [18] Then, on June 3, 1946, the United States Supreme Court provided Houser with both inspiration and opportunity to organize an action that was not limited to one locality. In what became known as the Irene Morgan decision, the court declared segregation on interstate bus travel unconstitutional.

At the time this decision was handed down, Rustin and Houser (who remained CORE's executive secretary) had just begun working as cosecretaries of the FOR's new Racial-Industrial Department alongside Muste at the New York office. Houser and Rustin decided to act upon the court's decision by sending a biracial group of experienced activists along interstate bus routes in the South. Houser hoped that this project would help foster a national agenda for CORE. He and Rustin also hoped that the action might spur the organizing of some cells in the South, where CORE had made no headway.

The original plan to ride from Washington, D.C., to New Orleans was scrapped when FOR members in the South warned against going into the deep South. Eventually, it was decided that a biracial group of sixteen would ride on interstate bus lines throughout the somewhat safer upper South for two weeks in April 1947.

Rustin and Houser, naturally, drew heavily upon fellow C.O.s for what they dubbed a "Journey of Reconciliation," the precursor of CORE's "Freedom Rides." Of the eight black men, Rustin and Wally Nelson had served time in prison during World War II. Five of the eight white men had been C.O.s during the war: Houser, Ernest Bromley, Igal Roodenko, Homer Jack (who would later help found SANE), and Jim Peck. Peck had joined CORE as soon as he was released from Danbury. He would be the only person to participate in both the 1947 Journey of Reconciliation and the 1961 Freedom Rides. Peck would also be beaten by segregationists on both occasions.

The Journey of Reconciliation traveled through Virginia, North Carolina, Tennessee, and Kentucky. Typically, the blacks would sit at the front while whites sat at the back of the bus. Technically, each was in violation of bus rules, but usually only the blacks were told by drivers to move. As anticipated, a number of tense incidents occurred throughout the trip. Fortunately, though, relatively little overt violence was directed at the activists. There were twelve arrests during the two weeks. In one incident, when Rustin and another black activist were being hauled off on charges of disorderly conduct, Peck insisted on being arrested alongside them. In Chapel Hill the following night, the arrest of Rustin and Roodenko held up the departure of the group's bus by two hours. During the delay in the bus terminal, Peck took some hard blows on the head from taxi drivers. The likelihood of greater violence led the group to flee town, aided by a sympathetic white minister.[19]

In flagrant disregard of the Morgan decision, the supreme court of North Carolina upheld the convictions of Rustin, Roodenko, and another participant for violation of local segregation ordinances. Due to limited funds, CORE asked the NAACP to appeal this decision, but NAACP lawyers decided the case as it had unfolded in state courts had become encumbered by technical legal difficulties that rendered appeal in federal courts a poor use of resources. Courageously, Rustin, the only African-American among the three, agreed to return to North Carolina to serve his sentence. He survived to publish his story, "Twenty-Two Days on the Chain Gang," in the *New York Post*.

The Journey of Reconciliation did not enforce the Morgan decision in the South, but it did enhance the prominence of CORE in pacifist and black activist circles. This had the intangible but significant effect of familiarizing a broad range of activists with the militant nonviolent ethos and the creative tactics of CORE protest, familiarity that helped change the tenor and add to the protest methodology of black freedom struggles beyond the small circle of CORE cadres. The 1947 Journey of Reconciliation also fostered the formation of more CORE cells, although these cells continued to direct their activities to local racial issues, primarily in the North.

WRL TAKEOVER

Other radical pacifists spent much of 1947 orchestrating a hostile takeover of the War Resisters League. The WRL had been started in 1923 by a Socialist New York schoolteacher, Jessie Wallace Hughan, to function as a secular counterpart to the FOR, which was nondenominational but explicitly Christian. Throughout the subsequent two decades, the WRL had limited itself to its original aim of educating people about pacifism, shying away from any form of direct activism. This had allowed it to weather many storms during the 1930s while other groups broke apart on the shoals of sectarian strife. Yet the WRL had a radical membership—more radical in outlook, overall, than the FOR, in part because the New York–based, secular WRL attracted many Jewish Socialist pacifists who felt uncomfortable with the FOR's Christian orientation.

It was natural for radical pacifists to take out WRL membership in the postwar era. The WRL and the FOR were the only sizable peace groups outside the Peace Churches at the

REBELS WITHOUT A REVOLUTION   57

time. Many C.O.s, though, still couldn't forgive Muste for co-operating with the CPS system during the war. The WRL was also more appealing to those radicals who advocated a secular Gandhism. By 1947, radical pacifists formed a sizable—and committed—minority within the WRL.

Dellinger and others began to eye the WRL as a worthy vehicle for furthering their radical pacifist agenda. The young men recently released from CPS and prison proved so dynamic and willing to attend so many meetings that they rapidly rose to take leadership roles in WRL after 1945. To further this development, leaders of the CNVR directed some of that group's resources to bolstering the influence of radical pacifists within the WRL. CNVR's office, for instance, sent out a mass mailing in 1947 to get its national membership to vote as a bloc in WRL elections.[20] Disciplined voting soon placed Dave Dellinger, Roy Finch, George Houser, Jim Peck, Igal Roodenko, and Dwight Macdonald on the executive committee of the WRL. This radical pacifist junta rapidly set about shifting WRL's orientation, passing, in June of 1947, a resolution that the WRL would now "adapt its literature and activities to the promotion of political, economic, and social revolution by non-violent means."[21]

This radical pacifist takeover of the WRL's executive committee led to a spate of resignations by the league's former leadership. Abe Kaufman resigned as executive secretary in September 1947. Resigning his position was a wrenching decision for Kaufman, who had been a student of Hughan's in high school and had served as WRL executive secretary for nineteen years. Four years later, when he took the further step of severing his membership in the WRL (which he would not rejoin until the 1980s), he explained his reasons:

> I have regretted the trend in the executive committee toward a "purist" or "absolutist" frame of reference which seemed to me would, at best, narrow the League to a small sect of self-satisfied persons. . . . At worst, . . . it would unnecessarily make the League and its members vulnerable (with justification) to charges of pro-communism, support of draft dodgers, and con-

ducting a conspiracy against the government. I had become
quite discouraged in dealing with people who place a premium
upon illegality of action. . . . I am often led to believe that some
of the executive committee are objectors to government almost
more than to militarism.[22]

Kaufman elsewhere stated: "I feel that the group in control of
the executive committee has destroyed the League's use-
fulness. . . . As long as the League continues its present effort to
be more than an educational organization and tries to enter the
arena of politics, it will find itself torn forever between support
of anarchistic impossibilists and alliance with Leninist communists."[23] Kaufman's criticisms show how little common ground
there was between the young fire-eaters fresh from CPS or
prison and the older WRL leadership. This helps gauge just how
radical the agenda of the former C.O.s was even in pacifist circles of the time. Direct action was anathema in the late 1940s
even to the leaders of the War Resisters League, the most secular
and socialist of the pacifist organizations that had come of age
before 1940.

The new slate on the executive committee promptly elected
Roy Kepler to succeed Kaufman. Kepler identified strongly
with the radicals, but he feared that the radical pacifist minority
was overzealous, using some of the strong-arm takeover methods so prevalent—and divisive—in Marxist organizations to
force their will upon a more moderate majority. "What I dis-
courage is the claim to exclusive truth and the only pacifism,"
Kepler wrote. "There has been a remarkable demonstration of
clinging to old delusions and stereotypes by people who pride
themselves on their liberation of thought and radical view-
points. The sectarian is evident . . . among the new secular and
radical fundamentalists."[24]

Kepler, who was by nature diplomatic and sensitive to diversity, tried to curb the arrogance of the militant insurgents
he led, encouraging them to reach out to WRL's traditional
membership. "I am not convinced," he wrote, "that the extension of new ideas or actions comes about when an organization

adopts as a policy a more direct method than its membership is really prepared to adhere to. . . . What I am suggesting is that the WRL at the present time is not in a position to expect its membership to share a civil disobedience viewpoint. . . . I believe in getting the revolutionaries before expecting the Revolution." [25]

Despite Kepler's best efforts, however, the executive committee steadily moved the WRL into the full radical pacifist program. By 1951, many long-term WRL members and almost the entire prior leadership had resigned from the organization, including Kaufman, Evan Thomas (brother of quadrennial presidential candidate and Socialist party leader, Norman), and WRL's founder, Jessie Wallace Hughan. The WRL has remained a radical pacifist vehicle ever since. Its executive secretary as of this writing is Ralph DiGia, who was in Danbury and Lewisburg during World War II.

PACIFICA RADIO

Roy Kepler soon tired of New York radical politics. While still working for the WRL, he returned to the University of Colorado to continue his studies that had been interrupted by the war. The deepening of the Cold War, however, led him to doubt the relevancy of his decision. By early 1948, Kepler was casting about for a new direction. In February, he sent a form letter to dozens of friends that included this dramatic flourish: "I am ready today to again give up my effort to finish my schooling in preparation for a career because I am fairly sure that unless a really great and dramatic effort, coming from the grass roots of the world, is not made, I'll never get much of a chance to take up a career nor will you to raise a family. I offer my full time and effort. Let the man with a family and a thousand dollars offer the thousand. This is not penny ante." [26]

Kepler found the new direction he sought in a response he received from Lew Hill. Writing from San Francisco (refreshingly far away from New York politics, in the opinion of both native westerners), Hill informed Kepler that his Pacifica Foundation was about to build its first radio station. "Before you walk up and down the earth with the devil in search of a cause, something big and daring," Hill chided, "I hope you will drop through San Francisco and go over the various things which are to be understood about Pacifica. Perhaps you would find it big enough."[27]

Kepler was soon ensconced in the Bay Area, working for radio station KPFA.[28] Hill's brainchild, the first listener-sponsored public radio station in the country, was designed as a vehicle to disseminate radical perspectives. The station's early years were consumed with a constant struggle to stay financially afloat, but gradually the listening audience grew, and that audience began to catch on to the idea that "listener-sponsored" really meant listeners had to send in money.

The eight hours of daily broadcast throughout the late 1940s and 1950s offered a fascinating hodgepodge of material. One hour every day was devoted to nonviolent children's programming. A typical broadcasting segment in 1957 included a choral concert, a children's story, a reading of editorials from British weeklies, a commentary by Dave Dellinger, and a live panel discussion devoted to the question, "How Much Nuclear Testing?" all within a three-hour segment.[29] KPFA became an important meeting ground for Beat counterculture and political radicalism in the Bay area during the 1950s. Not surprisingly, the Pacifica Foundation increasingly came under attack from people who were convinced it was a Communist front organization. When Pacifica attempted to grow from one to three stations in 1961, it found its licensing under careful investigation by the FCC. Eventually, the licenses were awarded, but Pacifica continued to be scrutinized by government agencies in subsequent years. After 1957, tragically, Pacifica no longer had the benefit of Lew Hill's brilliant guidance. Hill, who had long struggled with depression and a progressively debilitating arthritis of the spine, took his own life in 1957.

PEACEMAKERS

While Kepler and Hill were launching KPFA in 1948, Dave Dellinger and A. J. Muste were rolling the remains of the Committee for Non-Violent Revolution into a new, more modestly named group, Peacemakers. With Peacemakers, Dellinger and others largely dropped the last vestiges of mass-scale resistance rhetoric left over from the immediate postwar period to concentrate on creative techniques of small-group activism and alternative individual lifestyles. For several years after its founding, Peacemakers was the center of tactical and ideological creativity within radical pacifist circles, as Dellinger and his cohorts strove to sustain, implement, and even extend the radical pacifist vision amidst a political climate they found increasingly discouraging.

The 1948 "Call for a Conference on More Disciplined and Revolutionary Pacifist Activity" that led to the formation of Peacemakers was fairly standard radical pacifist fare, citing a "need of a more revolutionary pacifist program and the use of more effective and revolutionary action techniques" and reiterating the litany of commitments to direct action against conscription and segregation.[30] Initiated largely by Dellinger and Muste, the "Call" was signed by much of the radical pacifist leadership, including Bayard Rustin, George Houser, and Dwight Macdonald. The ensuing conference, held in Chicago in April 1948, was attended by two hundred people, of whom two-thirds were under thirty years old, many of them recent C.O.s.

Conference participants felt a need to start fresh with a new organization that would reflect the shifts taking place within radical pacifism. Organizationally, Peacemakers was designed to maximize participatory democracy. The group was organized into local cells that were nonhierarchical, made decisions by consensus, and were completely autonomous from the national leadership. In keeping with the new radical pacifist focus on small groups and individual revolutionary lifestyle, Peacemakers encouraged local cells to live communally and demanded an unusual degree of personal commitment from full members. A 1949 Peacemakers statement on terms for membership, for instance, used the word "discipline" five times in the course of its single page.[31] One Peacemakers pamphlet used the terms "disciplined," "thoroughgoing," and "total dedication" interchangeably.[32]

Yet within Peacemakers total dedication was a contested ideal. For Dellinger, it meant "right livelihood" in these years— a simple, nonconsumerist lifestyle based within intentional communities. For Muste and Rustin, it meant a reclamation of some aspects of their Marxist past. Muste, for instance, wrote of Peacemakers that "the kind of organization needed may perhaps be defined as a 'party' of the nonviolent revolution," adding for clarification that "the term 'party' is here used of a dedicated and active minority like the Communist Party, rather than the typical party in western democracies." Muste was quick to point out that he hoped Peacemakers, "in spirit, methods, and internal life, . . . would be practically at the opposite pole from the Communist or any other totalitarian or monolithic party," but he hoped Peacemakers members would emulate the commitment and collective discipline of Communist party members.[33] As the Cold War climate became evermore frigid in the early 1950s, Peacemakers' leadership articulated increasingly divergent responses to it. Tension would grow within Peacemakers between those, led by Dellinger, who felt a growing desire to pursue the implications of radical pacifism for personal spirituality and lifestyle, and those, led by Muste, who envisioned nonviolent cadres utilizing Communist-style group discipline.

The difference between these contingents, however, was one of emphasis. All agreed that Peacemakers should bare the teeth of radical pacifism. The national committee, some of its members showing familiarity with Tillich from their studies at Union, stated in 1948 that Peacemakers "cannot fail to keep non-violent resistance a central part of its program. . . . There is much truth in Paul Tillich's statement that the new is not born out of the old but out of the death of the old. It will be fatal if we become terrified or apologetic at being called 'negative.'"[34] Not shrinking from being labeled "negative" meant that Peacemakers was committed to drawing attention to itself and its causes by dramatic acts of symbolic confrontation with structures it deemed oppressive. One Peacemakers memo advised: "We ought not to strive to be spectacular by artificial means, but we should, on the other hand, refuse to be satisfied to be unnoticed."[35] Orchestrating symbolic confrontations—often, in fact, by "artificial means"—proved to be an essential method for a group that, a year after its founding, could only count 250 adherents, spread in cells from New York City to Palo Alto.[36] This impetus, however, kept Peacemakers vital as an experimental center for direct action tactics.

Peacemakers devoted most of its first year to fighting a reinstitution of the military draft during peacetime. In 1947, when the wartime draft legislation was drawing to a close, President Truman threw his support behind a proposed "Universal Military Training" (UMT) bill designed to maintain the combat readiness of the United States at a time when relations with the Soviet Union were rapidly decaying. Radical pacifists seized upon the prospect of a universal peacetime draft, at a time of rapidly expanding military budgets, as confirmation of their worst fears about the government's proclivities. A "Call to a Conference on Non-Violent Civil Disobedience to the Draft," signed by Dellinger, Houser, Kepler, Macdonald, Muste, and Rustin, stated unequivocally: "These recent measures are steps in preparation for atomic, bacterial, total war. . . . The adoption of a war policy by the United States, symbolized by the institution of the Draft, will therefore represent—unless the course is speedily reversed—the same turning-point in American development as was the advent of Hitler to power in Germany. It is the surrender to totalitarianism and degradation."[37]

Radical pacifists had never entirely discontinued draft resistance, because wartime conscription legislation had remained active to 1947 and because some C.O.s were still being held in CPS camps as late as 1947. Traditional pacifists, including the Historic Peace Churches, also now joined in opposing Universal Military Training. As early as 1944, traditional peace groups had made it clear that they would oppose a postwar draft, and the Peace Churches were determined not to repeat the CPS experiment, which they felt had proved untenable, if not an outright failure.

Throughout 1947, radical pacifists urged the burning of draft cards. While the response was not as large as organizers had hoped, the numbers were sufficient to be encouraging. At a protest in New York addressed by Dwight Macdonald, sixty-three cards were burned.[38]

Then in March 1948, Peacemakers gained an influential new ally when A. Philip Randolph, testifying before the Senate Armed Services Committee, announced that he would encourage draft-age black men to resist being drafted into segregated armed forces. Believing that an alliance with Randolph held the prospect for a mass-scale noncompliance campaign, Muste approached Randolph about joining forces under one organizational roof. Randolph and Muste still eyed each other warily in the wake of the MOWM plan for nationwide resistance to segregation, which Randolph had endorsed and then canceled five years before. Randolph felt he had been manipulated by Muste, while Muste felt betrayed by Randolph's equivocation. Now Muste insisted upon receiving from Randolph a firm commitment to see the campaign through before he was willing to dispatch Bayard Rustin and George Houser to work full-time with Randolph against conscription.

The resulting alliance of radical pacifist and Randolph forces was dubbed the League for Non-Violent Civil Disobedience Against Military Segregation. The league was led by Randolph, an arrangement Muste supported, believing that the league would be assured a higher public profile and deeper access to the black community with Randolph at the helm. Immediately after the formation of the league in June 1948, Randolph began urging young blacks and whites to burn their draft cards. Considerable hope prevailed in radical pacifist circles that they were on the cusp of a massive resistance campaign such as they had been seeking since the end of the war.

Less than two months after the league's founding, however, the alliance suddenly sundered. In the midst of his desperate election bid of 1948, President Truman sought to secure the black vote by issuing Executive Order no. 9981, effectively desegregating the armed forces. Randolph promptly called off all draft resistance on the grounds that Truman's order satisfied what he had set out to achieve. Muste and his allies felt that

Randolph had betrayed them yet a second time. Fingers were pointed in both directions. Randolph felt that radical pacifists were dissatisfied with anything short of revolution and manipulative in using issues such as the draft to further their revolutionary agenda. Randolph was quite right, of course, about the motives of radical pacifists, yet for Muste there was nothing inconsistent about using issues as levers to pry at American society in his quest for the nonviolent revolution he deemed necessary. Rustin criticized Randolph for giving an unwarranted primacy to race and failing to recognize that the issue of militarism was of equal importance. For Rustin in 1948, the issues of race and militarism could not be so easily uncoupled. He and other young pacifists felt Randolph had exposed feet of clay.[39]

Peacemakers, almost alone on the American Left, continued a campaign against UMT after Truman's order.[40] While the campaign was now limited to a few hundred faithful, indictments continued to be handed down in late 1948 and early 1949 against some draft-age men associated with the FOR and Peacemakers. Students in Kentucky, Minnesota, Pennsylvania, and elsewhere were sentenced to prison terms for refusal to register.[41] Glenn Smiley, a former prison C.O. who was now a member of Peacemakers and worked for the FOR, tried to organize more public draft card burnings in California. The risks involved in such organizational efforts became evident when Larry Gara, a Peacemakers member who had served two terms in the federal penitentiary as a C.O. during World War II, was ordered to undergo a psychiatric evaluation and sentenced to eighteen months in prison on June 2, 1949, for counseling a young draft resister to follow his conscience.[42] The steam that had been building up behind Randolph's leadership of the resistance campaign, however, could not be sustained by Peacemakers. Pacifists could claim no credit when UMT died quietly in Congress due solely to public war weariness.

With radical pacifists deprived again of access to a mass base after the split with Randolph, Dellinger began to steer Peacemakers back to lifestyle issues. Tax refusal increasingly became the lifestyle tactic of choice, providing a litmus test for members' moral purity at the nexus of the individual's economic relations to society. While individuals such as Thoreau had previously withheld taxes as a form of protest, Peacemakers in 1948 conducted the first organized campaign of tax refusal in American history. Tax resistance took a variety of forms, including merely earning less or only refusing to pay that portion of tax dollars that correlated to the percentage of the federal budget earmarked for military expenditures. Within Peacemakers culture, though, the highest honor was accorded to those who publicly announced an outright refusal to pay any taxes.

Muste displayed his usual flair for publicity when he joined the tax resistance campaign. To underscore his belief that Peacemakers' new line of action stood solidly within a long American tradition of moral witness against war, he sent to the Internal Revenue Service a copy of the gospels and Thoreau's essay, "On Civil Disobedience," along with a personal statement in 1951.[43] Such an assertion of Americanism demonstrated a savvy public relations sense at a time when McCarthyism was swelling toward its high-water mark. Muste found that he received little more than mild legal harassment from the government. In fact, he faced only minor legal hindrances despite continuing to publicly withhold taxes until his death in 1967.

Ammon Hennacy, an inveterate crank, was the consummate tax resister. It is only a slight exaggeration to say that Hennacy came to Peacemakers because he wanted to marry Dorothy Day. Day had been a member of the Industrial Workers of the World (the Wobblies) in the early 1900s before converting to Roman Catholicism. After her conversion, she creatively fused her new religiosity with her prior commitment to helping the poor. Together with Peter Maurin, an itinerant French philosopher, Day founded the Catholic Worker movement in the 1930s. The Catholic Worker printed a newspaper (that still sells for a penny per copy) and established intentional communal houses devoted to pacifism and to feeding and serving the needs of the poor in New York and other urban areas.

Day had a commanding presence that Hennacy found irresistible. He joined the Catholic Worker and Peacemakers, to the extent that Hennacy could ever be said to have joined a group, out of devotion to Day. Stories of Hennacy's endearing saltiness have become permanent fixtures in the Catholic Worker canon. Day politely brushed aside Hennacy's marriage proposals as an annual rite.

Hennacy trekked the country throughout much of his life, often working alongside migrant laborers for barely subsistence wages. Wherever he happened to find himself on April 15, he dutifully picketed the nearest IRS office with a placard announcing his refusal to pay taxes. Not surprisingly, one of Hennacy's books was entitled *One Man Revolution in America*. In lieu of paying taxes, Hennacy picked up trash as he walked along America's roads in order to fulfill his part of the social contract. Only once did federal agents attempt to garnish his wages. Hennacy simply arranged to be paid in food allotments rather than cash.[44]

Some Peacemakers, however, faced harsher repercussions than did Muste or Hennacy for their tax resistance. Art and Carolyn Emery, who lived at subsistence levels on a farm in Iowa, had their automobile seized and put up for public auction in 1951. Carolyn Emery went to the auction to personally confront her townspeople in the hopes of dissuading them from bidding. Emery's challenge must have been moving for some of her neighbors at the auction that day. Nonetheless, two people did purchase the car.[45]

CORE concentrated much of its energy on segregated parks and public pools in the North during the late 1940s. A general pattern emerged whereby interracial teams attempted to gain entrance to a facility, then refused to leave the area if denied admittance. Eventually, police would be called in, and the protesters would use the "scene" this created to get the attention of the local community. If the protesters were arrested, and especially if they were handled roughly by the police, some media coverage could be expected as well. This strategy was employed at pools in New Jersey, California, and Washington, D.C., in the late forties. The action at Anacostia Park in Washington, D.C., was an especially ambitious undertaking, because the CORE action followed upon a skirmish that had occurred when a group of black youths attempted to enter the pool there. When George Houser heard of this incident, he decided to make desegregating Anacostia the project for the Interracial Workshop he was holding in Washington that summer. The project succeeded, eased in part by the fact that the park was owned by the federal government.

Jim Peck led a much more protracted campaign during 1948 and 1949 at Palisades Pool in New Jersey. There, Peck was faced with an intractable owner and unusual brutality from park guards and local police. A number of protesters were beaten in the Palisades Pool campaign, but Peck suffered the worst beating, resulting in some broken bones.[46] Newspaper stories of these beatings contributed to the passage in 1949 of state legislation outlawing discrimination at swimming pools in New Jersey.

During this period, too, a new front was opening up that would be little appreciated, even by CORE, until events in 1960 shed new light upon it. In 1949, a CORE chapter in St. Louis started by Bernice Fisher began targeting lunch counters at Woolworth's stores for sit-ins. Utilizing impressive discipline and negotiating flexibly with store owners, St. Louis CORE succeeded in desegregating most downtown dimestores during its six-year campaign.[47]

VOICES IN THE WILDERNESS

Meanwhile, the Cold War was worsening. The Berlin Blockade of 1948 and the Soviet Union's detonation of an atomic weapon in 1949 prompted the United States to begin development of the hydrogen bomb. In 1950, a junior senator from Wisconsin charged that the State Department harbored over two hundred "card-carrying Communists." Also in that year, the Korean War began.

As the Cold War continued into the early 1950s and the Red Scare hysteria associated closely with Senator McCarthy intensified, groups on the Left suffered acutely. Radical pacifists found themselves placed in a difficult position by the Red Scare. On the one hand, they were strong advocates of civil liberties. On the other hand, there was no love lost between them and the Communist party, which was taking the full brunt of repression. Many still remembered the disruption caused in pacifist organizations by the cynical machinations of Communist front groups during the 1930s. In 1951, Muste again urged caution against allying with Communist fronts, warning that "Communist-inspired 'peace' campaigns are not genuine and that for pacifists to collaborate organizationally in such activities could only create confusion, . . . building up the Communist Party rather than pacifism or peace."[48] Muste suggested that a good litmus test for pacifists to apply when considering alliance with a peace group was to see whether the group's rhetoric criticized both the United States and the Soviet Union.

Despite their distrust of the CP-USA, however, radical pacifists took a principled and courageous public stand on behalf of the civil liberties of persecuted Communists. In 1949, for instance, the WRL and FOR disseminated an official statement that read: "Because of our consistent opposition to the [anti-Communist] Smith Act, we believe that the recent trial and conviction of the eleven national leaders of the Communist Party under the Smith Act was a regrettable event in our nation's history. . . . This is the very dictatorship and totalitarianism against which we desire to defend our country."[49] All radical pacifist organizations maintained this stand throughout the 1950s, a time when public declaration of concern for the civil liberties of those convicted under the Smith Act was a rarity on the American Left.

While radical pacifist groups were generally spared the government repression directed against other groups on the Left, their base of support nonetheless declined dramatically as the nation moved into a period of conservative consensus. The Fellowship of Reconciliation, the largest pacifist group in the country, sounded a note typical for pacifist groups when it reported in 1954 that its executive committee "took note of the dropping of 988 members, which brings us to the lowest membership total in the post-war period, 10,767." [50] And funding for pacifist activities was going the way of membership and public enthusiasm.

Struggling with isolation and decline, radical pacifists were able to mobilize little beyond small pickets in the opening days of the Korean War. Responding creatively to their limitations, though, the leaders of Peacemakers undertook an audacious media-grabbing action in 1951 that required only four protesters and little money. Bill Sutherland recalls that the plan originated when he and a small group of Peacemakers protesting the Korean War on a street corner were heckled by someone who asked, "Why don't you go and tell it to the Russians?" [51] Four Peacemakers who had been imprisoned together during the previous war—Dellinger, Sutherland, Ralph DiGia, and Art Emery (Carolyn's husband)—decided to express their opposition to both belligerents in the Cold War by taking their protest across the Iron Curtain. The original intention was to bicycle without passports from Paris to Moscow, protesting and passing out leaflets along the way. This plan reflected the utopian tradition of American dissent upon which radical pacifism drew. Acting within the world as if a higher reality were already present, the bicyclists intended to flagrantly ignore political boundaries. [52]

Sutherland, for one, felt that they were unlikely to get out of Paris without being arrested, but the bicyclists were able to ride relatively unimpaired as far as the Rhine. All the while, they distributed pamphlets printed in English, French, German, and Russian. Citing the traditions of Garrison, Tolstoy, and Gandhi, and invoking the support of "all international working class movements" and "all great religions," the pamphlets summoned an immediate worldwide movement of people refusing to participate in the Cold War. The pamphlets also attempted to dissociate the bicyclists from the policies of the United States government by emphasizing their prison history: "The U.S. you hear of most often is the U.S. of far-flung military bases, of atom bombs, of American dollars to bribe Europe into rearmament.

We are from another United States, a U.S. of persons who want peace and friendship and economic equality throughout the world. We ourselves have served prison sentences in the U.S. up to four years for opposition to militarism."[53]

Prevented from traveling farther East by opposition from Allied Command and the unwillingness of the Soviet Union to issue a visa to them, the bikers decided to illegally enter the Soviet-controlled sector in Baden, Austria. The staff of a Quaker center in Vienna attempted to dissuade them from taking this step. The Quakers told them of people who had disappeared in the Soviet sector and argued that the action might jeopardize the lives of Soviet soldiers who took the pamphlets. During their time in Europe, the four men had abstained from drinking alcohol, because Art Emery, a teetotaler, disapproved, and because they didn't feel it was a responsible way to spend the money donated for their protest. On the evening before entering Soviet-held Austria, though, they made an exception. Dellinger recalls Sutherland exclaiming, "By this time of night [tomorrow] we may be dead. . . . I don't give a damn what Art says. I'm having a beer."[54] Dellinger and DiGia joined him.

The next day, the four boarded a train with tickets to travel through the Soviet-controlled area of Baden to a British-controlled town on the far side. As the train pulled out of Baden after a brief stop, however, the four jumped off into the Soviet sector. They then split up to distribute their leaflets for several hours around the city. Sutherland attributes the fact that they were not arrested to the group's decision to hand out leaflets only to Soviet privates. "We were able to do it and get out of there before any higher-up could really figure out what was going on," he recalls.[55] Still, Dellinger remembers moments of fear, especially when Sutherland was late for the rendezvous. Dellinger, DiGia, and Emery worried that Sutherland, the only black in their group, might have been spotted as an American and arrested. At last, they saw Sutherland come around the corner. "Let's get out of here," he said. "I've never been so scared in my life."[56]

The Baden Action affirmed again the tactical insight Jim

Art Emery, Dave Dellinger, Ralph Digia, and Bill Sutherland, at the Rhine in 1951, during their attempt to bicycle from Paris to Moscow. Photo courtesy of David Dellinger.

Peck and other radical pacifists had learned from the Danbury desegregation struggle—that a small number of activists could grab headlines by audacious action. Newspapers around the world carried the story of the four pacifists who risked their lives to personally bring their opposition to the Cold War to Soviet foot soldiers. Yet beneath the apparent success of the European trip were signs of organizational desperation. The Baden Action maximized the leverage four men could wield over the media by staging a dramatic symbolic confrontation that made compelling news. Yet radical pacifists were forced to such creative measures in 1951 precisely because they were becoming accustomed to counting the turnout at their protests in single digits. Moreover,

The four bicyclists in 1990: Ralph DiGia, Dave Dellinger, Art Emery, and Bill Sutherland. Photo courtesy of David Dellinger.

the declining financial resources of radical pacifist organizations became painfully evident in the aftermath of the Baden Action. The bicyclists wanted to build upon their notoriety with further actions in Europe, but the combined resources of Peacemakers and the FOR could not sustain the four of them in Europe any longer. Reluctantly, Muste recalled them.

A gnawing sense of frustration and despair became evident in a meeting held by the Peacemakers executive committee shortly after the bicyclists' return. Discouragement brought long-standing divergences within the group to the breaking point. It was reported that the Peacemakers' six-month budget, including salary allocations, consisted of $1,000. Muste then opened the discussion with his assessment that "it seems altogether likely that building a radical pacifist movement of any size will be a tougher and slower job in the U.S. than anywhere else," citing strong nationalism, the continued popularity of the Second World War, and general affluence as factors. This was all a far cry from the optimism radical pacifists had felt in 1945. Dellinger's first comment was to ask, "What is the unique function of Peacemakers?" Four years after the group's founding, the executive committee could not offer a clear answer to this question. Here was a disappointed, disoriented, and burned-out group of activists who had been struggling together since 1940 and yet who had never felt further away from the revolution for which they yearned.

The meeting quickly broke down into the two basic orientations that had informed Peacemakers since its inception. Dellinger spoke for those who wanted to retreat into intentional communities, where members could experiment with disengaging themselves from the prevailing economic system and political culture. Muste, on the other hand, spoke for those who felt that Peacemakers should reorient itself along a more Marxist line, members rededicating themselves to group discipline and total commitment to nonviolent revolution. "If we have a program," Muste argued, "we won't have to be concerned about being cut off, going in communities. . . . There is nothing inherently wrong with certain of the methods the Communists use. Even though they have a revolutionary approach, they use the political party to spread ideas."

The meeting unraveled with a series of exchanges:

DELLINGER: I believe the building of communities is basic.
MUSTE: The building of communities is not necessarily a revolutionary approach. The AFSC [American Friends Service Committee] has used this approach but within the framework of the status quo. . . .
DELLINGER: Communities should be built by people interested in the Peacemakers movement. . . .
HOUSER: What does this mean for the individual? . . .

MUSTE: Communities cannot be an answer in and of themselves. . . . The only thing the nonviolent revolutionist can offer
is "blood, sweat, and tears". . . .
RUSTIN: This is getting us nowhere.

In his last remarks at a follow-up meeting the next week,
Dellinger spoke for them all when he ruefully stated: "Today
there is no place for rebels to go."[57]

Bill Sutherland and George Houser withdrew from American
activism shortly after these meetings, devoting their energies instead to promoting nonviolent strategies in Africa's freedom
struggle. Bill Sutherland left the United States to participate in
the pan-African movement based in Ghana. Later, he worked
for the government of Tanzania, where he makes his home today.[58] George Houser resigned from CORE in 1955 to devote
himself to the American Committee on Africa, an organization
he had founded in 1953.[59] Africa's freedom struggles became the
passion of his subsequent activism.[60]

CORE entered upon a period of disintegration. Bernice
Fisher declined to again lead the organization, devoting herself
instead to working within the Congress of Industrial Organizations.[61] CORE's summer workshops became defunct in 1954
due to lack of interest. Meanwhile, its affiliates languished. Only
four local cells sent representatives to the national convention
in 1955.[62] That CORE continued at all during this period was
due to the efforts of James Farmer and, especially, Jim Peck,
who continued to edit the group's newsletter, the COREelator.

Other radical pacifists went their divergent ways to sustain
and nurture their vision during the mid-1950s. A. J. Muste
strove to build new coalitions on the Left. Most of the tiny rem-
nant of radical pacifism, though, followed Dellinger's lead by
joining communal farms, entering into recuperative slumber.

Four

SLUMBER AND AWAKENING,

1952–1957

INTENTIONAL COMMUNITY

"Peacemakers will desire to order their lives in such a way that they achieve and share a maximum of community here and now," read the organizational statement in 1952. "Intentional community is, therefore, one of the basic items in the Peacemaker program—even in a sense *the* basic item."[1] Acting upon this desire for retreat away from the hostile political climate of the late 1940s and early 1950s felt by many Peacemakers, Dave Dellinger and Ralph DiGia founded a community in Glen Gardner, New Jersey. There, they found the countryside a bucolic balm for their wounded spirits. They also half-heartedly experimented with William Morris's nineteenth-century ideas for a handicrafts movement to offset industrial culture.[2] The most successful economic venture at Glen Gardner, though, was the launching of the Libertarian Press. The press churned out radical tracts, magazines, and even some books (including Ammon Hennacy's autobiography while he was living there).

76

Oddly, the press also published material for the local chapter of the Veterans of Foreign Wars. Dellinger played baseball with some of its members.[3]

Community living offered these radicals an opportunity to address personal emotional needs that some had neglected during the previous decade of imprisonment and activism. Dellinger found this period a time to work on his marriage, which had accumulated many tensions exacerbated by years of commitment, danger, and voluntary poverty. For Dellinger's wife, Betty, these stresses reached intolerable levels when Dave stayed away longer than expected to complete the European Action and when she learned that the men had risked their lives in Baden.[4] Dellinger recalls that gendered expectations contributed to this tension. He sometimes wondered why Betty was not more content to play the role of the homemaker while her husband was away on such business, and she, according to her husband, sometimes "succumbed" to wondering why he wasn't more effective at keeping the family and the community "out from under . . . crushing debts."[5] "The problem," Dellinger concludes looking back on those years, "was that all of us (men and women) had internalized the dominant sexual stereotypes of the society more than we realized."[6]

Much of the radical pacifist literature of the time bears out Dellinger's insight. It is indeed ironic, but not surprising, that these young rebels who prided themselves on challenging the social, economic, and political assumptions of 1950s consensus culture were remarkably mainstream in their gender assumptions. Radical pacifism, after all, emerged among all-male C.O. populations at a time when the ideal American male was a soldier. Subsequently, radical pacifist groups would always be male dominated, and much of the radical pacifist ethos for decades to come would conform to assumptions about male bravado and a puerile equation of manliness with male sexuality that these activists shared with American culture in general. One CNVR pamphlet that loudly proclaimed, "We must not be sidetracked! We must attack war and inequality directly!" opened with an implied connection between being sexually adult and being politically mature: "Some children don't know where babies come from. Some adults don't know what causes depression and war."[7] A similar connection between sexuality and resistance was drawn in the Peacemakers pamphlet, "An Open Letter to Young Men": "SEX is here to stay—and so is opposition to war!" The same pamphlet included male-gendered language about courage and nonconformity, recalled the ethos of American frontiersmen, and evoked images of male bonding—all in the name of draft resistance: "It is braver to resist tyranny than to submit to it. . . . Today a new type of bravery is needed— the bravery to resist public pressure and to pioneer for peace . . . in other words, the bravery to say NO to conscription and war, and to carry on non-violent struggle for total brotherhood."[8] Other examples abound. Typical of the linkage of libertarianism with manliness was the following from Peacemakers: "A man does not have to bow the knee to any other man, to the war system or any other institution. . . . In this age of conformity and regimentation and consequent sense of *impotence,* he can hold on to the fact that it is an essential mark of his manhood that he does not have to 'go along.'"[9] It is interesting that, in what they considered to be their most forceful pronouncements of opposition to the dominant culture, male radical pacifists were, in fact, replicating mainstream gender assumptions, a contradiction they shared with most of the male leadership of the Left at the time.[10]

Some of this male gendering carried over into the intentional communities of the 1950s. Decision making in these communities tended to be dominated by the male leadership. Ralph DiGia remembers that in the Glen Gardner community the men shared a natural camaraderie that came from being imprisoned together, whereas the women in the community did not share such a bond.[11] While Dellinger worked to repair his marriage during the years at Glen Gardner, there was not a serious challenging of sexual stereotypes in these rural communities. Daily chores tended to break down along traditional American family farm definitions of "women's work" and "men's work," although the men did participate in child care.

Not surprisingly, the two most family-centered programs undertaken by Peacemakers in the early 1950s were initiated by women. A Peacemaker Mutual Aid Fund to ensure financial support for families of imprisoned activists was begun by Margit Hirschenhauser. Similar concerns motivated Marjorie Swann during this period. Swann was the nearest equivalent to a female leader in radical pacifism. Growing up in Iowa and Illinois during the 1920s and 1930s, Swann became a pacifist early in her life. One important influence was the Methodist church her family attended, which was infused with Social Gospel assumptions. Growing up, Swann was also deeply influenced by direct, personal knowledge of the lingering destructiveness war leaves long after the fronts have grown silent. Throughout her childhood, Swann suffered physical abuse from her father, who had come back shell-shocked from the German front after the First World War. "Very early," she recalls, "I connected personal violence—family violence—with the violence of war."[12] Swann frequently went with her family to visit severely disabled soldiers at a local Veterans Administration hospital, visits that strengthened her abhorrence of militarism. Swann joined pacifist youth groups run by the Methodist church in the 1930s. During World War II, she worked at the National Committee for Conscientious Objectors. The NCCO had been established at Muste's urging to provide legal and other support to the prison absolutists. Swann began working at NCCO in a low-level position, but by the end of the war she became the de facto executive running the daily affairs of the organization, in part because most of the men in the office had been imprisoned. Under Swann's able leadership, the NCCO became a central clearinghouse for information about prison strikes during the war.[13]

Swann devoted much of 1953 to compiling a Peacemakers Directory. She was motivated by a desire to provide nurturance for individuals and security to families within the organization. Describing scenarios for which she imagined the directory being useful, Swann wrote: "If you're taking a trip into unknown territory, you would no doubt like to know where you could be sure of a warm welcome, food and a bed at little or no cost, and a discussion into the night with like-minded folk. . . . In case you're shipped off to prison, wouldn't it be a relief to know of a place where your family would be welcome for 'the duration'?"[14] While Swann's work on the directory was invaluable to married activists who risked imprisonment, her brand of movement domesticity was usually associated with women in radical pacifist groups and, consequently, largely devalued by the male leadership.

These intentional communities attracted a valuable young recruit to radical pacifism during the 1950s. Staughton Lynd was a recent college graduate who had been given an undesirable discharge from the military in 1954 due to his political views.[15] Son of the famous sociologists Helen and Robert Lynd,[16] Lynd and his wife Alice visited the Macedonia community in Georgia for a week during the summer of 1954 after having seen a slide presentation about it. The Macedonia community at that time had about half a dozen couples, of whom all the husbands but one had been C.O.s during World War II. Lynd felt that Macedonia offered a haven from McCarthyism. He and his wife Alice moved to Macedonia in November of that year, staying until late 1957, at which time they moved to the Hutterian Society of Brothers community in Rifton, New York, and then joined the community at Glen Gardner for six months. Staughton brought a well-trained, incisive, and sometimes caustic mind to the radical pacifist cause. Tom Cornell, who joined the Catholic Worker at about the same time and considers Lynd "one of the finest men ever," remembers that Lynd had "a sense of solidarity with the old radical tradition."[17]

Macedonia developed a reputation for tight-knit community life—so tight that individual growth was sometimes subsumed to the needs and demands of the collective. Glen Gardner represented another approach to community life. There, the focus was on individuals and nuclear families, resulting in less communal cohesion than at Macedonia. When the Lynds moved from Macedonia to Glen Gardner, they were struck by these contrasts. Staughton and Alice remember being at a birthday party at Glen Gardner when they noticed that some children were better clothed than others. Dellinger, Staughton recalls, was embarrassed that economic disparity existed in the community.[18] Yet Glen Gardner allowed more emotional breathing room for individuals and families than did the intense communalism at Macedonia. While Lynd may have been correct about Dellinger's embarrassment, Dellinger did not consider Macedonia's form of egalitarianism a desirable alternative.

Lynd and Dellinger articulated these differences in adjacent articles published in a new radical pacifist journal in 1957. Lynd's article was entitled, "The Individual Was Made for Community," while Dellinger's, predictably, ran under the heading, "The Community Was Made for Man." Lynd described the group life at Macedonia as disciplined but liberating. He acknowledged that some observers came away from Macedonia with the impression of "a certain bleakness, a closemindedness," but he argued that discipline was necessary to overcome selfishness and the "love-denying pattern" of American society. "The sense of all being . . . completely involved in the community life brought a deep joy" to Macedonia members, he argued.

Dellinger rejoined that "individuals should not have to abandon their privacy, their family life, their religious and intellectual freedom, in order to have the benefits of communal living." Dellinger cautioned that "not all aspects of the self are properly labelled 'selfish'" and concluded: "One must give one's self completely only to truth, or love, or God. The Community was made for man, not man for the Community."[19] The juxtaposition of these articles reflected a continuous tension in the intentional communities established by radical pacifists in the mid-1950s. It was difficult, if not impossible, for these libertarians to strike an easy balance with the demands of communal life.

RUSTIN

Bayard Rustin's life was destroyed and then rebuilt on new foundations in the 1950s. In January of 1953, Rustin was arrested in Los Angeles for having sex in a parked car with another man.

Dave McReynolds, a young Socialist then living in Los Angeles who was himself gay and had been influenced by Rustin's lectures on pacifism, went out to visit Rustin at the county farm where he was being held. McReynolds recalls that Rustin looked "terrible" and that he "knew it had destroyed his career."[20]

A. J. Muste promptly drummed Bayard out of the FOR. This cut Rustin to the quick: since the 1930s, the FOR had been his spiritual and political home, and Muste had been a powerful father figure for him.[21] Muste's ostensible reason for unceremoniously kicking Rustin out of the FOR, according to Bill Sutherland, was that his arrest might damage "the cause of radical pacifism," but Sutherland suspects Muste's hostility also stemmed from his puritanical views on sexuality.[22]

Within a week after Rustin's arrest, the FOR released an official statement that portrayed Rustin's sexual orientation as a moral failing. The statement noted that Rustin's job as a staff member was terminated, effective the date of his arrest. It went on to state that his "problem" had become known to the FOR staff only after 1941 and that it had been "seriously aggravated during his wartime prison experience." The course taken by the FOR leadership, the statement continued, had been to "counsel and help [him] to deal with his problem" while making it clear to him that his continuance on the staff depended upon his exercise of "rigorous discipline." "For some years," the statement noted, Rustin had been "growing spiritually"—that is, "until the unhappy recent event."[23]

Upon his return to New York, Rustin was given a staff position with the War Resisters League. The younger generation of radicals who ran the WRL were far more accepting of homosexuality than was the FOR leadership. Igal Roodenko, who was openly gay, had worked at the WRL for some years. Muste urged against the WRL's gesture. He resigned from the WRL's executive committee in protest when they hired Rustin. Ralph DiGia, who is now executive secretary of the WRL, remembers that Muste's behavior was "quite a blow to Bayard," one that Rustin "never forgot."[24]

Rustin continued to give eloquent speaking engagements for the WRL to small groups around the country. But those who attended these talks in 1953 or 1954 saw what appeared to be a ruined man: depressed and disheveled. By 1957, though, Rustin would be sporting new suits and a new air of confidence as a key player in the Civil Rights movement.

RECONSTITUTING THE LEFT

Muste and other radical pacifists who did not find rural communalism an appealing option continued to probe American consensus for signs of softness during this period. In 1955 and 1956, events at home and abroad began to suggest that the Cold War hysteria and rigid consensus of the early 1950s was beginning to make way for more diverse possibilities. Internationally, the death of Stalin in 1953 and the ascendance of Khrushchev in 1956 offered considerable hope for a thaw in the Cold War. On the domestic scene, Joseph McCarthy self-destructed and was censured by the United States senate in 1954. There was also a growing discomfort in American culture with the Procrustean bed of Cold War consensus. Rock and roll, James Dean, *Mad* magazine, and the Beat poets all came into prominence in the mid-1950s, evidence of an increased restiveness and irreverence, especially among American youth.[25] Yet more than youth were now questioning authority.

In July 1955, an appeal was published calling on all nations to transcend the immediate concerns of the Cold War and concentrate on the preservation of the human species. Signatories included Albert Einstein, noted British philosopher Bertrand Russell, and Linus Pauling (who had won the Nobel Prize in chemistry the previous year and would win a Nobel Peace Prize in 1962 for his work on behalf of nuclear disarmament). This appeal, and similar ones from prominent intellectuals that followed in quick succession, were catalyzed to a large extent by the increased potential deadliness of a superpower conflict in these years. In 1952, the United States detonated the first hydrogen bomb, followed quickly by the Soviet Union in 1953. The

"H-Bomb" increased the firepower of nuclear weapons by many orders of magnitude, rendering the "A-Bombs" dropped on Japan "firecrackers" in the parlance of Pentagon strategists. When it was still under development, Muste declared that "the hydrogen bomb has underscored and deepened the conviction . . . that war must be abolished if civilized life is to survive on this planet."[26] The "Einstein-Russell Appeal" showed that, five years later, influential intellectuals were beginning to share this assessment.

While increasing numbers of intellectuals were coming to concur with the long-standing pacifist position that failure of the superpowers to coexist boded mutual annihilation, this does not mean that intellectuals were becoming pacifists en masse. It is a recurring theme in the history of radical pacifism that the mass movements they had a hand in founding or even leading were not movements consisting primarily of people committed to pacifism. Rather, radical pacifists have only been influential in mass-based movements tapping increased public concern over a particular issue that also happened to dovetail with the radical pacifist agenda—such as race relations or the arms race or the Vietnam War. Radical pacifists in the late 1950s and 1960s were effective in stepping forcefully into such nascent movements because they maintained a hardy core of believers, tempered by considerable experience with nonviolent protest tactics, who were continuously active on issues of peace and justice and were always casting about for a particular issue that promised to generate a public groundswell against the status quo.

Radical pacifists began to act with more hope and confidence in the freer climate of 1955 and 1956. On the West Coast, Roy Kepler opened a bookstore near Palo Alto in 1955 devoted to the sale of paperback books. Paperback books as they are known today grew out of suggestions made by C. Wright Mills to a publisher for making first-rate books available to the average person. Kepler prided himself on having every paperback book in print available at his store until the sheer volume of paperback books made this impossible. Kepler's became a center of Beat, hippie, and antiwar culture in the Bay area, the southern point of a radical bookstore triangle that also included City Lights Bookstore in San Francisco and Cody's Bookstore in Berkeley. Kepler made national headlines for several years in the late 1950s because he refused to pay taxes on the store's sales. The Internal Revenue Service periodically threatened to close him down, but nothing ever came of it. For a time in the 1960s, Kepler would also be Joan Baez's business manager.

A. J. Muste, meanwhile, was determined to oversee the creation of a new, non-Marxist Left as the Cold War began to abate. In early 1955, he proposed the founding of a bimonthly magazine to facilitate thought on, as he put it, "the effort to constitute or reconstitute a non-totalitarian movement of the Left." Hoping to make the magazine an open forum for the Left, Muste's intended audience was far broader than just radical pacifist circles. The magazine, he wrote, "should try to reach out and speak to wide circles of students, labor people, Socialists, former Socialists and Communists, farmers, peace workers, pacifists, progressive church people."[27] Muste was able to entice Dellinger and some others who had spent the previous years in rural communes to help with the magazine, which was printed by Glen Gardner's Libertarian Press. Dellinger remembers the magazine venture as "the beginning of my permanent reconciliation with A. J."[28] Muste also reached out to Bayard Rustin, who agreed to join the editorial board. Dave McReynolds feels that Muste grew "on the Bayard issue," but he also believes that Muste had "a real self-interest in forgiving Bayard," since the two complemented each other so well that they "needed each other badly."[29] At any rate, Muste once again demonstrated his inimitable ability to reach across old disagreements to forge new alliances on the Left.

Thus was born *Liberation* magazine, which first went to press in 1956. Heir to Macdonald's *Politics* in its presentation of the most innovative social thought of the period, *Liberation* was rivaled only by Irving Howe's socialist magazine, *Dissent,* as the most influential little magazine of the Left in the second half of the 1950s.[30] Muste had from the start envisioned the magazine as "experimental and not dogmatic and doctrinaire."[31] The first issue of *Liberation* ran an editorial that struck a similar chord. The "failure of a new radicalism to emerge," it read, "is an indication . . . that the stock of fundamental ideas on which the radical thinking of recent times has been predicated is badly in need of thorough reappraisal."[32] This experimental orientation made *Liberation* a center for the exchange of ideas about a renewed Left. Historian Irwin Unger has stated that "the advent of *Liberation* and *Dissent* portended important changes in the political climate of the mid-1950s,"[33] while Lawrence Wittner claims that "a final crack in the seemingly monolithic facade of Cold War America developed with the founding of *Liberation*."[34]

Just a partial listing of *Liberation*'s contributors in its first two years of publication shows the vitality and eclecticism of the magazine: Sydney Lens, Michael Harrington, Paul Goodman, Martin Luther King, Jr., E. D. Nixon, Lewis Mumford, and William Appleman Williams. Yet *Liberation* remained unmistakably a radical pacifist magazine. The editorial board of the first issue read like a list of the guiding lights of Peacemakers, including Muste, Dellinger, Finch, and Rustin, with DiGia working as business manager. Later, Staughton Lynd and Dave McReynolds would be added.[35] While the list of contributors over the years was diverse, the articles that appeared in the magazine maintained a decidedly radical pacifist bent. To the extent that *Liberation* was a germinal contributor to the forging of a new American dissent, it was at once an important vehicle for disseminating the radical pacifist agenda and the most important contribution made by radical pacifists to the intellectual content of the American Left.

While Muste was founding *Liberation* in 1955, Dorothy Day of the Catholic Worker was organizing direct action against the arms race across town. Since 1951, a New York City ordinance had required citizens to take shelter during an annual civil defense drill. At a specified time, air raid sirens would eerily sound across the city in an exercise designed to prepare the citizenry for nuclear attack. Those who remained out of doors were subject to arrest. Critics, among them some liberal faculty at Columbia University, argued that such drills were more palliative

Dorothy Day. Photo by Diana Davies, reprinted with permission from the War Resisters League files.

than protective, pointing out that most of the "shelters" in the city would be wiped out in a nuclear attack. There was also a general discomfort with the authoritarian nature of the ordinance. Day utilized these sentiments brilliantly when she organized a simple but resonant symbolic protest. In June of 1955, she invited a group of radical pacifists to remain sitting on park benches outside City Hall in defiance of the drill. Among the twenty-seven protesters joining Day that afternoon were Muste, Dellinger, DiGia, Rustin, and Peck. For refusing to take shelter, the protesters were arrested, capturing national media attention and raising a debate about the ludicrous nature of civil defense in the nuclear age. Day decided to make her civil defense protest an annual event. Each year the number of protesters joining her grew until the ordinance became unenforceable when more than two thousand people resisted the drill in 1962.

THE CIVIL RIGHTS MOVEMENT

While these developments were taking place, the most dramatic reawakening of American dissent in the 1950s grew out of the battle against segregation. By 1954, radical pacifists increasingly viewed southern race relations as a promising area for activity. Black communities in the South were growing increasingly restive under the daily constraints, indignities, and terror of the segregation system. Then in May of 1954 the Supreme Court handed down perhaps its most important ruling of the twentieth century, declaring segregated schools unconstitutional in the landmark *Brown v. Board of Education of Topeka, Kansas* case. Hope that segregation could be effectively challenged, and that such challenges would receive the support of the federal government, surged through the black communities of the South after the *Brown* decision. What historian Aldon Morris has termed "movement centers" began to cohere around indigenous leadership in southern cities as black activism increased, often sporadically, throughout 1954 and 1955.[36]

The FOR decided to rejuvenate its organizing efforts in the South in 1954. A memo of that year proposed that the FOR reestablish its southern office, which had been closed in the early 1950s, and send field workers to devote two years to renewed race work in the South. The FOR also planned to send its National Field Secretary to work in the South after the ground had been laid for a renewed FOR presence there: "At the end of this two-year period," the memo read, "it is expected that Glenn Smiley (who is now opening regional work in the new Great Lakes region) would be ready to spend a year in the South, building on the achievements of these workers."[37] By coincidence, then, Glenn Smiley had been preparing since 1954 to spend a year in the South working intensively on race relations, a plan that landed him in Montgomery about a month after the boycott against segregated buses began.

Smiley was well-suited for southern race work. A white Methodist minister raised in Texas, Smiley understood the nuances of southern race relations. As a white minister, Smiley was able to engage in dialogue with other white ministers on behalf of the black community and even attend Klan meetings to ascertain what white supremacists were planning during times of increased tension. Smiley also brought to his work in the South an intimate familiarity with the direct action ideology and tactics radical pacifists had developed and honed over the previous fifteen years.

Smiley had been on the FOR staff since 1942, when he held a pulpit in Redlands, California. He joined the FOR due, in part, to the influence of Bayard Rustin, whom he had first heard speak in 1941. Smiley also joined CORE when it was first founded in 1942 and remained an active member until the 1960s. During the 1940s, he participated in a number of CORE actions in southern California. Smiley went to prison in 1945 rather than register for the minister's exemption, although he was married with three children at the time. After being paroled, he became the National Field Secretary for the FOR.[38]

In November of 1955, Smiley was dispatched by the FOR to provide any assistance he could to the town of Orangeburg, South Carolina. Agitation against segregation by black leaders there had led to a boycott of white businesses. Whites responded with a counterboycott. The FOR contact letter apprising Smiley of the situation noted that the white counterboycott was threatening the food supply of local blacks and that the situation was very delicate.[39]

Shortly after arriving in Orangeburg, Smiley wrote back to

the FOR office that he "found an almost total lack of communication between groups in the city . . . , in spite of the fact that about a dozen people have lost their jobs, families have been refused delivery of milk and bread, and some threats to life and property have been received."[40] A naturally diffident person with a keen sense of southerners' distrust of outsiders (especially outsiders representing a group based in New York), Smiley devoted his efforts to providing assistance to local movement leadership and facilitating dialogue between whites and blacks rather than trying to insert himself or the FOR into a leadership position. His first task was to arrange an unpublicized meeting of black and white ministers to break the ice in communication. He also arranged for literature on nonviolence to be passed out in the black community, a tactic that would become standard FOR practice in southern cities engulfed by racial struggle in subsequent years. Although the Orangeburg situation dragged on for years with no clear-cut resolution, Smiley's work there proved pivotal in averting what could have been a tragic outcome. Among his other successes in Orangeburg, Smiley managed to convert Matthew D. McCollom, the black minister who led desegregation forces in Orangeburg, to a commitment to nonviolence. McCollom later wrote that Smiley's efforts prevented the Orangeburg situation from erupting in violence and probably saved McCollom's life.[41]

Meanwhile, what had been intended as a one-day boycott against segregated seating on city buses in Montgomery, Alabama, unexpectedly gave rise to the classic phase of the Civil Rights movement. Under the leadership of E. D. Nixon (longtime member of Randolph's Brotherhood of Sleeping Car Porters), Rev. Ralph Abernathy, college teacher Jo Ann Robinson, and other local organizers, Montgomery's black community was ripe for a challenge to segregation in 1955. The bus system seemed a natural target, since it was a service used at one time or another by most blacks in the city. In March of 1955, the anticipated boycott of buses was almost organized around fifteen-year-old Claudette Colvin after she refused to give her seat to a white passenger. At the last minute, however, it was decided that Colvin would not be an effective protest symbol, since she was several months pregnant. Then, on December 1, 1955, Rosa Parks, a seamstress widely respected in the black community, made a stand similar to Colvin's on a city bus. A one-day boycott of all city buses for the following Monday was promptly heralded from leaflets and every black pulpit in the city. Black organizers formed the Montgomery Improvement Association (MIA) to oversee the boycott. For a variety of reasons, the older black leaders in the city thought it expedient to give the titular leadership of the boycott to the twenty-six-year-old doctor of theology who had moved to Montgomery in the spring of 1954 to assume the coveted pulpit at Dexter Baptist Church. Much to everyone's surprise, as the boycott mushroomed into an extended showdown with the white power structure of the city, Martin Luther King, Jr., emerged as the actual leader of the MIA and, for increasing numbers, a national symbol of African-American resistance.[42]

A few weeks into the boycott, as the potential significance of the Montgomery situation became clear, the WRL and the FOR dispatched separate radical pacifist emissaries to consult with the MIA. This duplication of effort was a direct result of Rustin's arrest. The WRL sent Rustin while the FOR sent Smiley to offer aid to the leadership of the MIA. FOR leaders did not feel Rustin should be sent at all to such a delicate situation; they were especially concerned that the Montgomery police might try to discredit the MIA by targeting Rustin as an outside agitator who was homosexual and had once belonged to a Communist youth league.[43] Nevertheless, Rustin arrived in Montgomery as the WRL emissary on February 21, while Smiley arrived a few days later.

Rustin and Smiley found a determined but struggling leadership in Montgomery. No one had expected the boycott to become a sustained confrontation, and the black leadership felt unsure about how to maintain interest, discipline, and hope in the black community over the long haul. The considerable experience with nonviolent resistance Smiley and Rustin brought gave them immediate access to the boycott leadership upon their arrival in Montgomery, although many of the MIA leaders remained wary of these outsiders.

Smiley and Rustin both admired King enormously from the start. In his first letter back to FOR's national office from Montgomery, Smiley spoke warmly of King's promise: "Martin Luther King is a grand guy. . . . At first King was asked to merely be the spokesman of the movement, but as sometimes happens, he has really become the real leader and symbol of growing magnitude. If he can really be won to a faith in non-violence there is no end to what he can do. Soon he will be able to direct the movement by the sheer force of being the symbol of resistance."[44]

Smiley carried a pile of books about nonviolence to his first meeting with King. When Smiley commented offhandedly that he assumed King was familiar with the work of Gandhi, King surprised him by responding that he had only a passing familiarity with Gandhi's ideas.[45] Smiley handed over the books he had brought and began to discuss with King the tactics and ideas of nonviolent resistance.

King had also been having similar discussions with Rustin prior to Smiley's arrival. Smiley wrote after his first meeting with King that "Bayard has had a very good influence on King, wrote the much quoted speech of last week, and was in on all the strategy," although he added cryptically: "Wish we had Bayard of the old days in this." Smiley also wrote back to the FOR office that he felt "I have a good 'in' with him [King], and he has asked me to come back. He expressed interest in some of the ideas I presented, so last night I wrote him a letter, enlarging upon those ideas and adding some more that he might use in the mass meeting tomorrow night."[46]

King's "pilgrimage to nonviolence" was advanced but not completed when the Montgomery bus boycott began. Despite his humble disclaimers in his first meeting with Smiley, King, in fact, brought more than a passing acquaintance with Gandhi's ideas to his leadership. King had heard Muste speak on nonviolence in 1949, when King was a student at Crozer Seminary, although hearing Muste did not at the time convert King to pacifism.[47] King also attended a lecture on Gandhi given by Mordecai Johnson, president of Howard University, in 1952. Johnson's "message was so profound and electrifying," King later wrote, "that I left the meeting and bought a half-dozen books on Gandhi's life and works."[48]

King had publicly advocated nonviolent discipline in the early days of the boycott, weeks before the arrival of radical pacifists from the North. These early articulations represented King's own amalgam of nonviolent principles, deeply informed by his Christian beliefs.[49] The clearest—and noblest—example took place on the evening of January 30, 1956, when King's house was bombed by segregationists. After being assured that his family was not injured, King addressed an outraged crowd of blacks gathered in his yard. Standing on his porch, King spoke in the language of Christian nonretaliation, urging the crowd to disperse peaceably.[50]

King's faith in the efficacy of pacifism, though, was not absolute prior to the boycott. In his last year at seminary, King had found his belief in Rauschenbusch's Social Gospel theology shaken to its roots by his first encounter with Niebuhr's Christian Realism in classes taught by Kenneth Smith. Smith and Ira Zepp would later write that Niebuhr "burst like a bombshell into King's liberal theological-ethical world view."[51] Looking back on this crisis of his theological assumptions years later, King wrote: "Niebuhr helped me to recognize the complexity of man's social involvement and the glaring reality of collective evil. Many pacifists, I felt, failed to see this."[52]

Whether due to theological uncertainty or a more visceral desire to protect his family, King's ambivalence about the efficacy of the nonviolence he had preached from his porch after the bombing became evident when, just two days later, he applied for gun permits to arm bodyguards at his home.[53] Shortly after Rustin arrived in Montgomery, according to historian David Garrow, Rustin saw a pistol lying on a seat in King's house. When asked about it, King responded that it was only to be used in self-defense. Rustin stayed up late into the night urging King to reject retaliatory violence as a method.[54] Smiley, too,

was concerned about the potential for violence in the Montgomery movement, writing back to the FOR office in his first
letter from Montgomery that King "wants to do it right, but is
too young and some of his close help is violent. King accepts,
as an example, a body guard. . . . The place is an arsenal. King
sees the inconsistency, but not enough. He believes and yet he
doesn't believe. The whole movement is armed in a sense, and
this is what I must convince him [King] to see as the greatest
evil." [55]

Despite the fact that a gathering in New York of Norman
Thomas, A. Philip Randolph, and FOR leaders decided to urge
Rustin to leave Alabama and that Smiley had been advised not
to even meet with Rustin so as to avoid any association,[56] Rustin
and Smiley in fact met together to share ideas from the first day
Smiley arrived in Montgomery. The two, after all, had worked
together in radical pacifist circles for many years. Sharing notes
but working separately, Smiley and Rustin devoted themselves
to advising King on nonviolent tactics. Smiley wrote to New
York that "King runs out of ideas quickly and does the old
things again and again. He wants help, and we can give it to
him without attempting to run the movement or pretend we
know it all." [57]

As it turned out, Rustin did have to skip town on February
28 after a journalist threatened to expose his past, leaving Smiley
as the principal representative of northern pacifist groups in
Montgomery. Rustin continued to provide King regularly with
tactical advice, and he ghost wrote an article for King that appeared in *Liberation*,[58] but he could no longer have a day-to-day
presence in Montgomery, as Smiley did.

While it is impossible to gauge the relative weight of Smiley's and Rustin's contribution to King's political development
during the boycott, the considerable tactical experience they
brought to their discussions with the young King no doubt
helped convince him that nonviolence could be an effective
movement method; and consideration of the efficacy of nonviolence appears to have been key to King's ultimate embrace of
nonviolence as "a commitment to a way of life." [59]

At any rate, it is clear that King's thinking about nonviolent resistance evolved rapidly during the boycott. King later wrote that "as the days [during the boycott] unfolded, I came to see the power of nonviolence more and more. . . . Many of the things that I had not cleared up intellectually concerning nonviolence were now solved in the sphere of practical action."[60] In March of 1956, Rustin reported enthusiastically that King "is developing a decidedly Gandhi-like view. . . . He is eagerly learning all that he can about non-violence."[61] Noting that pacifists had long wished for a revolutionary situation such as Gandhi faced in India, Smiley wrote exuberantly in early March that a "full-scale revolutionary situation" existed in the South and that he was "thrilled with the potentialities of the leadership of their youthful Negro Gandhi."[62]

Smiley also played an instrumental role in facilitating dialogue in the Montgomery situation, much as he had done in Orangeburg. In May of 1956, he organized a meeting of fifty ministers from Alabama to discuss race relations in general and the Montgomery situation in particular. In that same month, he arranged a private meeting in Atlanta of King, Abernathy, and other leaders of the MIA with the leadership of the FOR. Muste felt it was "the most significant [conference] I have attended in fifty years in the Christian ministry."[63] Smiley commented of this and similar meetings: "Not since the first days of World War II have I participated in such eager discussions of pacifism."[64] Smiley also led a number of nonviolence workshops in Montgomery during 1956. In these workshops, he introduced MIA members to the role-playing methods that CORE had used so effectively in preparing participants for conflict situations.

The Montgomery bus boycott lasted over a year, but, in the end, the "Walking City" broke down segregationist recalcitrance. In December of 1956, the United States Supreme Court finally mandated that Montgomery's bus lines be desegregated. On the morning of December 21, the first busload with desegregated seating pulled out from a Montgomery terminal. Martin Luther King, Jr., sat in the front of the bus. Glenn Smiley sat in the place of honor beside King.

The black freedom struggles of the 1950s and 1960s emerged largely from within the communities of black America. And the leadership of that movement drew deeply upon resistance traditions that inhered in African-American culture. Yet radical pacifists Smiley and Rustin made significant contributions to the nonviolent tactics of the forces King led in the Civil Rights movement. It is true that King brought concepts of nonviolence to his leadership from the start, and he certainly synthesized the secular Gandhism of radical pacifism with his own Christian iconography, drawing deeply upon the black Baptist tradition of his youth and the Personalism he had studied as a graduate student. Yet Rustin and Smiley bequeathed to King the wealth of tactical experience gained by radical pacifists since World War II, in the process informing King's conclusion that there was a viable nonviolent path to a successful outcome in the boycott.

As the Civil Rights Movement gained momentum beyond Montgomery, King undeniably became the leader who most gave form and substance to the revolution sweeping the South. His continued espousal of nonviolence ensured that the orthodox methodology of the movement remained nonviolent direct action at least through the mid-sixties. For many in the Civil Rights struggles, to be sure, nonviolence was at most a tactical convenience for use by a people with little formal political power. For King, however, the Montgomery experience had made nonviolence a tenet of faith.[65] In fact, one white radical pacifist who worked with King in the early 1960s felt that few among the leaders of the Southern Christian Leadership Conference cared about nonviolence, but that King kept the SCLC to an espousal of nonviolence because of his leadership qualities.[66]

Smiley's influence in the Civil Rights movement declined rapidly after the Montgomery boycott, although he remained on good terms with King. Smiley had always maintained that it was not the role of the FOR to attempt to lead the Civil Rights movement, but, as he wrote in one report from Montgomery, to "service" incidents.[67] He referred to the FOR's role as that of "initiator and trainer,"[68] and he expected the FOR to play a smaller part as the black freedom struggles burgeoned.[69] Groups in the black freedom struggles also rapidly moved toward all-black leadership as part of the process of empowerment in the late 1950s and early 1960s. At any rate, while Smiley continued to confer with King, he clearly no longer held a position in King's inner circle after the Montgomery campaign.

Rustin, on the other hand, identified the emerging Civil Rights movement as his new institutional home in the aftermath of the Montgomery boycott. Although King kept him out of the limelight due to the potential embarrassment his past might cause the movement, Rustin nonetheless remained King's closest advisor until the mid-1960s. To many who had known Rustin in the years following his arrest in Los Angeles, he appeared in the late 1950s like a man who had been given a new lease on life. Yet long-term associates also noticed something disturbing in the new Bayard: a singular focus on civil rights and a growing disdain toward radical pacifist groups (which he would later refer to as "a tiny band of fervent white initiates").[70]

Rustin's new dismissive attitude toward radical pacifist organizations was evident at the formation of the Southern Christian Leadership Conference. In the aftermath of the Montgomery campaign, there was considerable interest in forming a new regional organization to attempt to generate a Civil Rights movement throughout the South. At the FOR's behest, Smiley had initiated a few small meetings to discuss the possibilities for such an organization. These early efforts were overshadowed in early 1957, however, when Rustin organized a meeting in Atlanta to present his plans for a Southwide movement. From this meeting, to which Smiley was not invited, the Southern Christian Leadership Conference emerged.[71] Rustin envisioned the SCLC as an organization capable of leading southern blacks into mass-based action—a base, he argued, radical pacifist organizations could not possibly deliver. Whereas the FOR had proposed little more than a replication of the Montgomery experience in other southern cities, Rustin's model for southern black activism was more akin to the union struggles of the 1930s and the March on Washington Movement of the 1940s. Not surprisingly, he sought to ally the SCLC with A. Philip Randolph, who had organized the all-black Brotherhood of Sleeping Car Porters as well as the MOWM. Although he had once worked under Muste's direction to try to change Randolph's March on Washington Movement into a biracial organization, Rustin was now instrumental in establishing the SCLC with an all-black leadership, arguing that only a black leadership would appeal sufficiently to the masses of southern blacks. It is impossible to say how much Rustin's new politics may have been influenced by a resentment toward Muste's FOR for abandoning him when he was arrested. What is clear, at any rate, is that Rustin's new criticism of northern pacifist groups as inadequate allies for the emerging Civil Rights movement would have policy ramifications for the SCLC in the 1960s, when Rustin vehemently advised King to stay focused on racial issues and avoid making public pronouncements against the Vietnam War.

The years from 1952 to 1957 saw a remarkable series of shifts in the hopes and fortunes of radical pacifists. Bayard Rustin felt his world crash around him, only to be rebuilt with even greater promise, in unexpected ways and on somewhat different foundations. Dellinger and several others retreated from the onslaught of McCarthyism into rural recuperation, only to find themselves drawn back out into the world by signs of a thaw in Cold War consensus and the concomitant possibilities for renewed activism. Muste had been convinced all along that the answer lay in unflagging coalition building and relentless agitation. As the cultural glaciers of the Cold War began to break apart in the mid-1950s, a few intrepid radical pacifists led by Day and Muste had stepped up their activism with civil defense actions and the launching of *Liberation* magazine. Then the Montgomery boycott, more than any other event, convinced many radical pacifists that Muste was right: the times were, indeed, propitious for nonviolent direct action—perhaps even for the birth of a new Left.

Five

NUCLEAR FALLOUT

Just before sunrise, the hills were lit by a blinding flash. Slowly, as nineteen pacifists looked on, a mushroom cloud rose to towering heights above a military installation in the Nevada desert. Eleven of those observing the detonation had been arrested for trespassing on the base the previous day, August 6, 1957, the twelfth anniversary of the atomic bombing of Hiroshima. After being released later from a local jail, Lawrence Scott, Jim Peck, Albert Bigelow, and eight other trespassers joined Muste outside the base just in time for the predawn explosion. One of the group remembered that, looking into the plume of a hydrogen bomb, "our conviction was made firm that it would be infinitely better to suffer death by a nuclear bomb than commit the blasphemy of dropping it on other men."[1] Jim Peck wrote that "it was as if you were to see a certain monster in your dreams and then one day were suddenly to come upon it in reality."[2]

Albert Bigelow had become a pacifist exactly twelve years

before the day of his arrest. Born into a wealthy Boston family, Bigelow had attended Harvard before entering the navy. During World War II, he served with distinction as captain of a ship in the Pacific. When he first learned of the atomic bomb dropped on Hiroshima, however, Bigelow immediately concluded that modern war is morally unsupportable. This belief was later confirmed for him when he and his wife housed survivors of the Hiroshima blast who had been brought to Boston for reconstructive surgery.[3]

Bigelow and the others had come to Nevada in the summer of 1957 as members of a group led by Lawrence Scott, a Quaker pacifist. Scott's activism stretched back to the 1940s. He had worked with James Farmer on desegregation issues in 1941 and had participated in CORE's Kansas City local in 1943. He had also attended the founding conference of Peacemakers in Chicago in 1948 and since 1954 had worked for the American Friends Service Committee in Chicago. In 1957, Scott left the AFSC because the organization would not support his decision to resist tax payments.

Scott had become increasingly concerned about the dangers to world health posed by fallout from nuclear testing. In early 1957, he wrote an article (later published in *Liberation*) entitled "Words Are Not Enough," in which he called for bold action against nuclear testing and blasted the "effete, middle-class Friends [Quakers] of today" for not doing enough against the arms race. Articulating a long-standing radical pacifist assumption, Scott called for a privileging of action over analysis, asserting that "speaking words has become so cheap in this age that only the literal act has much meaning."[4]

In April 1957, Scott organized a meeting in Philadelphia of pacifists interested in active opposition to nuclear testing. Among those in attendance was Homer Jack, a World War II prison absolutist who had worked closely with George Houser in Chicago during the early 1940s. The Philadelphia group decided to meet again in Washington the following month at the Prayer Pilgrimage for Freedom organized by Martin Luther

King, because the pilgrimage would draw activists from around the country. Before King delivered the keynote address to a crowd of about thirty thousand, a group of pacifists and liberals met in a small office to discuss Scott's ideas for a campaign against nuclear testing. It was at this meeting that Muste suggested the Nevada Action for the upcoming anniversary of the Hiroshima bombing.

Out of these two meetings in April and May of 1957, two organizations emerged that were designed to have separate but complementary tactical foci. One group was to push forward the radical pacifist agenda, concentrating on direct action. Originally named Non-Violent Action Against Nuclear Weapons (NVAANW), it later became the Committee for Non-Violent Action (CNVA).[5] The other group was to reach out to the middle class and intellectuals by pursuing more moderate avenues of challenging above-ground nuclear testing. This group, led by Norman Cousins, editor of the liberal *Saturday Review* was called the Committee for a Sane Nuclear Policy (SANE). Homer Jack, active in the leadership of both organizations, would become the de facto organizational link between these two groups established in tandem by a coalition of radical pacifists and liberals in 1957.[6]

Scott had touched a nerve with a public increasingly concerned about the effects of nuclear fallout. Despite official assurances that fallout from the above-ground nuclear tests being conducted by the United States, the Soviet Union, France, and Great Britain posed no health risks, increasing numbers of people feared that the "experts" were misleading them. SANE, using moderate methods to tap into a growing public fear of nuclear fallout, grew at an expansive rate. By July of 1957, SANE's leaders were able to present President Eisenhower with a petition signed by ten thousand people asking for a test ban.[7] Even more dramatic was the response to a full-page advertisement taken out in the *New York Times* by SANE on November 15, 1957, calling for an end to nuclear testing. Thousands of letters flooded SANE's office, and by the following summer it

could boast 130 chapters and 25,000 members.[8] In the late
1950s, SANE became synonymous in the popular mind with
the campaign against nuclear testing.

Meanwhile, Scott was busy organizing SANE's radical pacifist
fraternal twin. He and Muste organized the action against the
nuclear test in Nevada for August of 1957. The following year,
CNVA engaged in its most influential action when Bigelow and
three other CNVA members (Orion Sherwood, William R.
Huntington, and George Willoughby, who had been imprisoned as a C.O. during World War II) attempted to sail a thirty-
foot ketch they had christened the "Golden Rule" into a re-
stricted zone in the Marshall Islands where the United States
military was scheduled to detonate a hydrogen bomb. In the
Gandhian tradition of openness, Bigelow announced his intentions ahead of time. He even published an article on his intentions the previous February.[9]

The "Golden Rule" managed to sail from San Francisco as
far as Hawaii. While docked in Hawaii, however, a judge issued
a restraining order demanding that the crew not leave port to
continue to the Marshall Islands. Bigelow, who was captain of
this ship, hesitated, prompting Muste to fly out to Honolulu to
urge him to defy the judge's order. Bigelow finally agreed and
set out from port with his original crew and a late addition,
Muste. They got less than a mile out from shore before being
intercepted by the Coast Guard.

The "Golden Rule's" crew entered a plea of guilty when
arraigned in Honolulu on May 7, 1958. Bigelow, Willoughby,
Huntington, and Sherwood gave eloquent statements at their
arraignment about the dangers nuclear weapons posed to humanity. CNVA's leaders at this time carefully crafted their public
statements to address concrete issues, such as the health effects
of nuclear fallout while avoiding more controversial ideological
issues such as pacifism or the radical politics motivating many of
CNVA's members.[10]

After the crew received suspended sentences, Bigelow

placed a large sign on the stern announcing that the "Golden Rule" would set sail again at noon on June 4. Because Bigelow and Huntington were the only crew members with navigational skills, the group decided to keep Huntington in reserve on shore. Huntington's replacement was Jim Peck, who had been in Hawaii throughout the action for just such a contingency.

Ten minutes before their planned departure on June 4, federal marshals arrived to arrest Bigelow, who was addressing a crowd of journalists, well-wishers, and curiosity seekers. After Bigelow's arrest, Huntington rejoined the crew, and the "Golden Rule" snuck out of port. This time, they managed to get about three miles out from Honolulu before two Coast Guard vessels turned them around. All crew members except Peck (who had only violated the injunction once) were now given sixty-day jail sentences. One journalist quipped that jail was now the "Golden Rule's" home port.[11]

The "Golden Rule's" dramatic confrontations grabbed national headlines in 1958, much of it sympathetic to CNVA. *Newsweek* ran a long article on the protest in its religion section, and the *Boston Herald* referred to the crew's actions as "Thoreauesque." Protests in support of the action took place across the United States.[12] The generally favorable reporting of the action can be attributed in part to Bigelow's credentials as a patriot during World War II and to the middle-of-the-road statements made by Bigelow and Muste, which kept to the issues SANE had helped to make mainstream concerns, the health dangers of fallout and the fear of nuclear war. The crew members also garnered respect from some journalists and sections of the general public for their clear willingness to risk death at sea to convey their message.

To the surprise of everyone, including CNVA organizers, the "Golden Rule" action did not end with the imprisonment of its crew. The most dramatic event of the action occurred aboard another ship owned by Earle Reynolds, an anthropologist who had done fieldwork for the Atomic Energy Commission in Hiroshima after the war but who had no connection with CNVA whatsoever. Reynolds and his family were sailing around the world in 1958, when, by coincidence, they docked in Honolulu during the "Golden Rule" controversy. Attending the trial of the crew members, Reynolds became convinced that CNVA was right. Without prior announcement, he and his wife slipped out of Honolulu to complete the voyage of the "Golden Rule" aboard their own boat, the "Phoenix," an appropriate name from the perspective of those in CNVA who thought the "Golden Rule" action had ended with the imprisonment of Bigelow and his crew. The Reynolds family managed to sail several miles into the South Pacific zone marked for nuclear detonation before they were apprehended by the Coast Guard. The image of an entire family ("average" Americans, as opposed to "professional" activists) risking their lives in this way to complete the "Golden Rule's" mission was tailor-made for media consumption. Earle Reynolds went on a national speaking tour that included numerous radio and television appearances.

Despite their failure to effect military policy or even prevent the single detonation in the South Pacific that the action had targeted, CNVA's leaders considered the "Golden Rule" action, in its ability to command sympathetic publicity, a success beyond anything previously attempted by radical pacifists. As a result, there was considerable discussion within CNVA about what to do for an encore. These discussions exacerbated tensions that had already developed between an older, more cautious leadership and a younger, more combative group within CNVA. Scott and Bigelow argued that the "Golden Rule" action proved CNVA could reach more people on specific issues such as nuclear testing if the organization avoided jarring the political sensibilities of middle-class Americans. The younger group within CNVA advocated "upping the ante" with more militant action and rhetoric, which better expressed the urgency they felt about the nuclear arms race. These younger militants within CNVA coalesced around a "wildcat" project in Wyoming in 1958. This project drew sustenance from a new militancy that was emerging among American youth in the late 1950s.

The Cheyenne Project began in early 1958, when two

young activists, Ted Olson and Art Springer, presented to the CNVA leadership a plan to disrupt the ongoing construction of ICBM missile silos in Cheyenne, Wyoming. Olson and Springer hoped to move CNVA beyond its focus on the public health dangers of above-ground nuclear testing to a more controversial challenging of the morality of possessing a nuclear arsenal. In the process, they hoped to shift CNVA's tactics from moral witness of the "Golden Rule" variety to a far more combative attempt to prevent construction of a nuclear installation. This tactical departure, termed "obstructionism," faced stiff opposition within CNVA. While it was harmonious with many radical pacifist pronouncements of the late 1940s, some radical pacifists in 1958, who were still savoring the invigorating tonic of favorable media treatment received by the "Golden Rule" after the arid years of the McCarthy period, opposed the Cheyenne Project. Others, such as Scott and Bigelow, felt that obstructionism was not in the best tradition of pacifism, insofar as it set up a confrontation based in part upon physical rather than moral coercion.

Wary of developments on the most militant wing of CNVA, Scott refused to back the Cheyenne Project, claiming that the organization's resources were already stretched too thin to take on such an action.[13] Undeterred, Olson and Springer proceeded to organize the action in CNVA's name without official organizational sanction. A flurry of letters went back and forth between Scott and the planners in Wyoming during the weeks prior to the action. Scott wrote to Ted Olson on July 22 that he was "very disturbed" by news that Olson and Springer were proceeding with plans for a project on a scale never approved by the organization's leaders. He pleaded with Olson to recognize "the serious nature of the mistake you are making." Scott argued that the American public would not support a civil disobedience campaign against the installation of ICBM silos, and he feared that "misuse" of civil disobedience might "discredit that method and leave a bitter fruit."[14] Subsequent letters only confirmed how far Olson and Springer were from Scott in their perceptions about the amount of preparation and discipline required for nonviolent activism, about the need to consider the political sensibilities of the general public, and about the likelihood that the facility in Cheyenne could actually be shut down.[15] Olson and Springer raced ahead with their plans despite Scott's remonstrations.

In early August of 1958, participants in the Cheyenne Project began to prepare the local community for their action by passing out leaflets. Far from building goodwill with local residents, many of whom worked at the military base, the leaflets intensified animosity toward the project by questioning the humanity of those who worked on missile deployment. Demonstrators first attempted to obstruct the entrance to the base on August 18. They were easily removed, but they returned the next day even more determined to prevent trucks from entering the site. During the day, protesters were removed from the roadway dozens of times in tense confrontations. Trucks drove right up to the protesters before slamming on their brakes, behavior that many of the protesters believed was encouraged by military authorities. Then, late in the afternoon, Ken Calkins, a graduate student at the University of Chicago, suffered a fractured pelvis when he was hit by a truck at the entrance to the base. Calkins spent ten days in a hospital before beginning a jail term for trespassing. After the arrests of August 19 and the injury to Calkins, the Cheyenne Project faltered. Springer at this point negotiated a deal with Scott to have CNVA carry the financial and organizational burden of quickly wrapping up the project.[16]

Scott himself went to Cheyenne to oversee the project's end. He wrote back to Willoughby, Muste, and Rustin that his situation was difficult because young people continued to arrive on the scene from San Francisco intent upon continuing the confrontation at the base. Scott respected the intentions of these young men and women: "All of these people are solid, rational people with deep convictions," he noted. "The act of Ted [Olson] and Ken [Calkins] . . . spoke to their condition and they are ready to give their life if need be to make the same manner of witness." Yet Scott also felt that the young activists he confronted in Cheyenne "care little about whether this builds a

peace movement or has any political relevance or communica-
tive value." [17] As late as September 6, as young activists continued to arrive, Scott was still having difficulty preventing further
obstructionist actions at the base in his organization's name.
Scott was becoming deeply worried about the course this new
activism was taking. "In the present situation at Cheyenne," he
wrote, "I think that non-violent obstruction is immoral, in-
effective and has the character of non-violent coersion [sic]. I
am concerned because its use in Cheyenne may set a pattern for
the peace movement in America, or split our efforts into holier-
than-thou fragments." [18] Eventually, Scott was able to close out
the Cheyenne Project. The action had received very little public
attention and had even had negligible effect on construction of
the missile installation, but the Cheyenne Project touched off
an intense internal debate over obstructionism within CNVA.

Brad Lyttle, one of the participants in the action at Cheyenne, rapidly developed a reputation as the most influential
apologist for the obstructionist camp within CNVA. Although
he was only thirty years old at the time, Lyttle brought considerable knowledge of pacifist activism to his role as challenger to
Scott's influence within the organization. Lyttle, whose father
was a Unitarian minister and whose mother was a pacifist and
Socialist, had been raised in a home where Socialist party leader
Norman Thomas was a frequent dinner guest. He was, he recalls, "brought up in a pacifist atmosphere." In high school, he
refused to stand for the national anthem, and, when he heard
over the radio that Hiroshima had been destroyed by a single
bomb, Lyttle, then eighteen, instantly felt certain that humanity
now faced the stark, apocalyptic choice between continued war
and survival. Lyttle enrolled at Earlham College, a Quaker
school, in 1945. During his college years, he roomed with James
Otsuka, whose studies had been interrupted by time in a CPS
camp, and he developed a close friendship with Corbett Bishop.
After graduation, Lyttle struggled to decide between pursuing a
career in medicine and devoting his life to pacifism. He concluded that the presence of nuclear weapons made activism the
more urgent vocation. When he was drafted for the Korean War

in 1953, Lyttle refused to report for alternative service and was sentenced to a year and a day. After his release from prison, Lyttle spent eighteen months traveling the world to study peace movements, visiting Gandhian ashrams in India as well as peace groups in Europe and Southeast Asia. Lyttle joined the Cheyenne Project shortly after his return to the United States in 1958.[19] His considerable experience in pacifism and his fiery zeal to end the arms race soon catapulted him to the leadership of those within CNVA who felt that the approach advocated by Scott and Bigelow was unnecessarily tame.

Lyttle's style was radical pacifism in a new key. Believing that nuclear Armageddon was imminent, he told other activists that they should sacrifice their personal lives to devote every ounce of energy and use every nonviolent tool at their disposal to prevent nuclear holocaust. Some radical pacifists who had themselves been castigated in the 1940s by traditional pacifists for being too urgent now leveled similar criticisms at Lyttle.

Lyttle wrote vigorous essays defending obstructionism as a method that had moral, religious, and political legitimacy.[20] He argued in *Liberation* that the hostility the activists encountered in Cheyenne was not a failing of the action but a sign of the "exceptional power of the educational technique of nonviolent obstruction." Lyttle, in other words, felt that obstructionism evoked hostility because it forced people to confront the disturbing possibility of nuclear war. He argued that pacifists should not be averse to upsetting the public, concluding: "Much of the weakness of the peace movement is due to anemia caused by too much middle-class prudence. . . . We must think and act on the assumption that we can bring about a nonviolent revolution against the tradition of military power."[21]

In the late summer of 1958, CNVA's future direction hung in the balance between Scott's supporters and the obstructionist contingent, increasingly led by Lyttle. Muste, who held enormous prestige in both camps, tipped the scales in Lyttle's favor. In September, he wrote to Scott: "My feeling about the debate between yourself and Ted Olson about 'obstruction' tactics is that you tend to see one important aspect of the problem but to emphasize it too strongly at times to the neglect of the other aspect. . . . Ted sees and feels the compulsion on himself and possibly others not to omit any act which places not only his words etc. but his body . . . against the atrocity which is being perpetrated. If he were throwing himself in the way of a madman seeking to hurt a child no one would question that this was genuine nonviolent resistance and not obstruction in the derogatory sense of the term."[22] Muste also circulated a memo within pacifist circles arguing that he was "quite unable to see" any "fundamental" moral difference between the "Golden Rule" and Cheyenne actions, even if the latter did involve a higher degree of confrontation.[23]

Muste's backing was enough to swing other radical pacifists—and, with them, CNVA—in line behind Lyttle. This change in direction eventually led Larry Scott, the founder of SANE and CNVA, and Albert Bigelow, CNVA's most famous member, to resign from the organization.

This was a shift of some moment for radical pacifism as well as for CNVA. In backing obstructionism, Muste and those who followed his lead reaffirmed the radicalism of their pacifism. They resisted the lure of respectability that had enticed CNVA after the "Golden Rule" action received such favorable and widespread coverage. In returning to their familiar prophetic stance, of course, they also returned in some sense to the desert of obscurity. For CNVA would never again command media attention even remotely as it had when it used more moderate tactics and ideologically cautious statements during the "Golden Rule" action. The shift in favor of obstructionism showed once again that radical pacifists privileged individual cathartic action over pragmatic efficacy. The eclipse of moderates such as Scott and Bigelow by obstructionists also exhibited radical pacifism's tendency to follow small victories with increased militancy, a tendency that would plague activism against the Vietnam War. On the other hand, Muste's decision to back Lyttle and his youthful followers placed the radical pacifist leadership at the end of the 1950s squarely on the side of the younger generation's confrontational militancy—a decision that would allow middle-aged radical pacifists to forge strong coalitions with youth movements during the 1960s.

Muste backed up his words in 1959 by participating in a CNVA action that included obstructionist methods organized by Lyttle, Homer Jack, and Muste himself at an ICBM installation outside Omaha. After weeks of leafleting and other activities by CNVA members in the Omaha area, the seventy-four-year-old Muste and two other men initiated civil disobedience at the missile site on the first of July by climbing over a fence onto military property. CNVA periodically sent small groups of two or three people onto the base to commit civil disobedience over the next several weeks, while supporters maintained a vigil outside. Muste violated his parole by returning to participate in the vigil. Brad Lyttle was arrested on July 8 and, like Muste, served a prison sentence for violating his parole after returning to the protest. On July 13, two of the younger participants attempted to obstruct the highway leading into the ICBM installation. All told, fifteen people committed civil disobedience in the Omaha Action between July 1 and August 10.[24] The Omaha Action had a negligible effect on the public debate about the arms race, but as an action with official CNVA sanction it did have the effect of solidifying CNVA in its support of obstructionist militancy.

Omaha Action's organizers, however, were surprised to see how much attention the media paid to Marj Swann, the long-time Peacemakers activist who, along with Lyttle, Muste, and others, served a prison term for violating her parole immediately after trespassing onto the base. What set Swann apart was the fact that she was the mother of four young children. Such behavior challenged assumptions about decent maternal behavior that were widely held in the late 1950s.[25] Swann's treatment by the legal system and the media focused on whether she was a fit mother in choosing to go to jail despite what were perceived to be her domestic responsibilities. The judge who sentenced Swann lashed out at her during the proceedings in heavily gendered terms, calling her "an irresponsible, irrational, stubborn, foolish woman" and a "bad mother."[26]

Even articles sympathetic to Swann strove to reconcile her political radicalism with mainstream popular notions of maternal decorum. Jhan and June Robbins, freelance journalists who were experienced at conveying gender issues in the popular press (with such page turners to their credit as "129 Ways to Get a Husband" and "Forty-Nine Ways to Make Marriage More Exciting"),[27] wrote sympathetically of Swann's pacifism in an article in *Redbook,* but they hastened to portray her as a consummate mother and homemaker. Far from being hardened or otherwise defeminized after doing time in the penitentiary, for instance, the Robbinses assured readers that Swann "slipped back quickly into her normal household routine. A pile of mending awaited her. She went to P.T.A. meetings and pushed her basket at the supermarket, nodding to friends and neighbors."[28]

Swann herself employed traditional gender images to support her radical agenda. The day after being sentenced, Swann wrote from prison that her concern for what the arms race meant for children motivated her actions: "And to children— all children—can we say we would not suffer that they might live? . . . The children must know that we care enough."[29] She similarly called upon the language of maternal love as a justification for her activism when she explained to *Redbook* readers: "I love my children dearly. . . . I know that if there is another war—a nuclear, global war—they will die. So will millions of other children all over the world." Vividly connecting quaint images of child care in the home with public activism on global political issues, Swann added that for ensuring the safety and security of children "cod-liver oil and clean diapers and even good-night kisses are less important right now than stopping the H-bomb."[30] Swann's politicization of images of female domesticity was remarkably similar in style to Women Strike for Peace, an organization founded two years later.[31]

TOWARD A NEW LEFT

Throughout this period in the late 1950s, Muste was trying to foster dialogue and build coalitions in an effort to forge a new

Left. Viewing CNVA as just one aspect of this broader venture, Muste became increasingly interested in harnessing the growing restiveness among students. Toward this end, Muste became particularly active in personally bridging the radical pacifism of the 1940s to the student activism of the late 1950s and 1960s.

In 1956 and 1957, Muste organized a series of meetings under FOR auspices to facilitate dialogue on the non-Communist Left, efforts historian Maurice Isserman considers "the first and most publicized attempt at regroupment" of the American Left after the McCarthy era.[32] In May of 1956, Muste organized a gathering in Carnegie Hall of several hundred representatives from a broad spectrum of the non-Communist Left. W. E. B. DuBois, Roger Baldwin, and Norman Thomas were among the speakers in what participants generally considered a fruitful exchange. Muste also organized a similar meeting in Chicago the following October. These meetings were then formalized in 1957 at Muste's initiative as the American Forum for Socialist Education. The forum sponsored gatherings throughout 1957 at which virtually every thinker of influence on the Left participated, including Max Schachtman, Irving Howe, C. Wright Mills, and I. F. Stone, as well as radical pacifists Muste, Rustin, and young Dave McReynolds. The forum broke down within two years under the weight of high-profile government investigation and due to internal sectarian strains, but during its short time of influence the forum managed to get disparate radical groups in America to consider new opportunities for cooperation on issues of peace and social justice, displaying yet again Muste's lifelong penchant for getting leaders with considerable defensiveness and egotism to talk together.[33]

One of the direct links between the radical pacifism of CNVA and the new student Left was the Student Peace Union, founded by Ken Calkins in 1959, a year after Calkins had fractured his pelvis at the Cheyenne Action. SPU spread rapidly to campuses. Its famous slogan, "No Tests, East or West," reflecting radical pacifists' critique of both belligerents in the Cold War, appealed to many students critical of the arms race. In one month during 1960, SPU was able to gather ten thousand signatures on a peace petition distributed at colleges.[34] During the first few years of the 1960s, SPU was the central organization for white student activism. As such, it became a vehicle by which the radical pacifist approach was disseminated to the next generation of student activists. By 1964, however, SPU was eclipsed by the Students for a Democratic Society (SDS), a group which had worked closely with SPU on peace issues in the early 1960s.[35]

In 1960, Brad Lyttle also built an important link between the radical pacifists in CNVA and student activists when he initiated the Polaris Action. Lyttle first conceived of the project while in prison for his participation in Omaha Action. Reading an article in *Time* magazine about the destructive power of the new Polaris nuclear submarines, Lyttle quickly concluded that direct action against the centerpiece of the navy's nuclear program in the congested suburban area where the subs were being built would draw international attention. With Muste's support, Lyttle set up an office near the Groton, Connecticut, shipyard and organized a leafleting campaign. Lyttle himself was knocked unconscious by an angry shipyard worker while leafleting, and CNVA had to maintain an around-the-clock watch to protect the action's office, which had had every one of its windows broken within the first week of operation. This embattled action soon began to draw young activists, who engaged in daring acts of protest. Demonstrators, for instance, sailed a flotilla of skiffs out into the estuary in an attempt to obstruct a Polaris submarine's maiden voyage. One protester swam out and clambered aboard the sub's hull, generating a memorable picture of an individual at considerable personal risk placing his body against a black behemoth of the Cold War. Tom Cornell, a young member of the Catholic Worker whose great-grandfather had helped develop the first military submarine in the United States, remembers that in a related action his boat got caught in currents and unintentionally drifted into a submarine. Putting out his hand to prevent a crash into the sub's hull, Cornell felt strong emotions as he came "in physical contact with a machine that could incinerate all of Europe in a flash." When he returned to shore, Cornell burned his draft card as an act of "withdrawal from the system." Although he had been classified as a conscientious objector, Cornell no longer felt he could "recognize the legitimacy" of the government's classification. Cornell would go through about a dozen draft cards by the end of the decade.[36]

Lyttle recalls that the Polaris Action was marked by a full measure of pacifist analysis, commitment, and action. It was, he feels, "the best pacifist project I've ever participated in."[37] Tom Cornell, who credits Lyttle with having "thought up or executed more than half of the project," concurs that "there wasn't any departure from nonviolence" in the Polaris Action. Cornell recalls that organizers would even welcome FBI agents at meetings in the spirit of adherence to a principle of openness.[38]

At the same time CNVA was attracting student protesters to Lyttle's Polaris Action, the organization's fraternal twin, SANE, was self-destructing due to a failure to remain attuned to the changing tenor of the times. SANE's troubles began when Senator Dodd of Connecticut attacked the group, claiming that it harbored Communists among its leadership. Norman Cousins promptly capitulated to Dodd's allegations by purging the organization of any former or suspected Communists. Cousins, himself vociferously anti-Communist, feared that Dodd's attack would alienate SANE's moderate liberal membership if strong action to keep the organization impregnable to red-baiting were not taken. Yet, in capitulating to Dodd in 1960, Cousins unexpectedly appeared more as a relic of a bygone phase of the Cold War than as a leader of a progressive antinuclear organization. At the dawn of the 1960s, with the Communist party in the United States moribund, liberals were inclined to agree with Leftists that the excesses of anti-Communist campaigns represented a graver threat to American democracy than did domestic communism. Cousins had expected to preserve the support of moderates; to his astonishment, he watched helplessly as the liberal center of SANE melted and the organization became a pariah on the Left in the aftermath of his purges. Cousins would still have his moment in the sun—notably, when President Kennedy included him in the negotiations for the Atmospheric Test Ban Treaty in 1963—but by that point Cousins led a disemboweled organization.

The demise of SANE in 1960 was a clear signal that the tide in American politics was shifting to the left. There is every reason to believe that a principled resistance by Cousins to the Dodd inquiry would have significantly strengthened SANE. Muste, for one, lambasted Cousins for failing to take the pulse of the nation. "What has happened in SANE," he wrote in *Liberation*, "is tragic, partly because . . . it need not have happened. Everything in our political life shows that we are at a turning point and that Americans sense it. . . . [If SANE had stood up to Dodd], such an attitude might have called forth a tremendous response; might have put new heart into many people, especially young people fed up with conformism and apathy."[39]

This experience led Muste to become a strong and early advocate for a policy of nonexclusion in organizations of the Left during the 1960s. Nonexclusionists such as Muste frankly stated that Communists could participate in protest coalitions because they had become largely irrelevant on the Left. This policy cut through much of the red-baiting that had hamstrung organizations such as SANE and allowed for the building of coalitions that, as with Muste's American Forum, had usually broken down over sectarian questions of which stripes of Marxists to exclude.

Although they could not know it in 1960, Muste's nonexclusion policy later allowed radical pacifists to play a central role in organizing mass demonstrations against the Vietnam War. By building an inclusive tapestry of organizational alliances for specific actions, they would be able to periodically call into the streets a wide spectrum of groups that often agreed on little but their opposition to the war in the late 1960s.[40] Nonexclusion, however, would also prove to have a dark side, as many on the Old Left foretold. Nonexclusion made it nearly impossible for responsible leaders to control fringe insurgent forces within co-alitions. When this danger was more fully actualized in 1968 and 1969, the consequences for the Left would be disastrous.

More than anyone else, Muste was able to mine the full potential for coalition building that nonexclusion offered. Freed to a degree from red-baiting and the full force of sectarianism in the early to mid-sixties, Muste was able to call upon a lifetime of personal relationships on the Left in bringing people together. Muste was a skilled negotiator who worked with stamina at meetings to find some common thread between groups highly suspicious of each other. Muste also had kept older radical pacifist groups attuned to the concerns of the new student Left by swinging CNVA behind Lyttle's obstructionist policies. Muste's New Left ethos made him a vital link between the Old Left and the student leadership of the New, who tended to dismiss the previous generation of activists. Writing in the *Nation* about the student leadership of the New Left in 1965, Jack Newfield commented that "the few older figures whom the new generation seems to respect come out of the radical pacifist tradition—men like . . . the 80 year old A. J. Muste."[41]

The cross-fertilization these alliances facilitated was reflected in the pages of *Liberation* during the 1960s. Frequent contributors included Tom Hayden, Paul Booth, Carl Oglesby, and Todd Gitlin of the Students for a Democratic Society (SDS) as well as Jerry Rubin and Marty Jezer of the Yippies. *Liberation* also published a blueprint for society penned by the Diggers of the Haight-Ashbury counterculture and several early feminist and gay critiques and manifestoes, including a germinal feminist memo written by women in the Student Nonviolent Coordinating Committee. As the rapidly shifting shoals of activism demanded continual communication between contingents in the 1960s, *Liberation*'s radical pacifist editors became central figures in the discourse on the Left. Also clear in the magazine's pages, however, is the fact that Muste, Dellinger, Lynd, and the other editors did not simply march to the tunes of young radicals but maintained their commitment to Gandhism, often gently re-

monstrating activists who seemed to be veering impatiently toward an advocacy of violent confrontation.[42]

FREEDOM RIDES AND PEACE WALKS

While Lyttle's Polaris Action, Day's air defense protests, and
Muste's coalition building all strengthened ties between radical
pacifists and students in 1960, what riveted the attention of activists that year was the sit-in movement begun by black students
in the South. During 1958 and 1959, the Civil Rights movement had experienced a lull in activity after the promising mid-
1950s. In the last two years of the decade, King's SCLC had
struggled to keep the momentum of the racial revolution going;
they knew the powder keg was there, but they couldn't strike
the right spark. Then, unexpectedly, match was put to fuse in
1960 by a group of students in Greensboro, North Carolina,
who decided to engage in a sit-in at a local dimestore lunch
counter that did not serve blacks. Within weeks, the sit-in
movement was rocking the South, with the rest of the country
watching intently. Young activists like Tom Hayden were enthralled by the bravado of the student-led movement.

Media coverage at the time portrayed the students as acting
with complete autonomy. There was some truth to this por-
trayal, insofar as the students were not part of a central organization and there was a strong element of spontaneity to the pro
tests. Yet the influence of CORE certainly permeated the
students' activities. Historians Meier and Rudwick point out
that the Greensboro students were influenced by a sympathetic
white businessman who had read Houser's *Erasing the Color
Line*.[43] In that pamphlet, Houser outlined sit-ins at Woolworth's
lunch counters conducted by CORE members in the late 1940s
and early 1950s.

CORE soon did more than simply serve as a model for the
sit-ins. The inexperienced student leaders of the ad hoc movement soon received consultative and institutional support from
CORE as well.[44] CORE quickly dispatched two experienced

organizers to Greensboro and, through its network of local cells, initiated a national boycott and picketing campaign against Woolworth's. CORE's close identification with the sudden upsurge of student activism redounded to a resurgence for CORE, which had felt sidelined during the most prominent racial struggles of the 1950s. Its linkage with the sit-in movement and with the student organization that would emerge in October of 1960 from that movement, the Student Nonviolent Coordinating Committee (SNCC), would catapult CORE into its period of greatest prominence.

CORE gave concrete aid to the sit-in movement. Jim Peck, who had been reared in New York mercantile society, took a prominent role in organizing white liberal support behind the boycott of Woolworth's in the North. Peck also represented CORE in the first negotiations with Woolworth executives to discuss desegregating their facilities in the South. CORE's leaders also called upon their local chapters to spread the sit-ins to as many southern cities as possible. Just twelve days after the initial sit-in at Greensboro, a CORE group sat in at a Woolworth's in Tallahassee. This chapter was not unprepared, for they had engaged in a similar sit-in at a local Sears in 1959.[45]

Rejuvenated from their mid-1950s stupor by their involvement with the determined young men and women leading the sit-in movement, CORE, led by Farmer and Peck, decided to reprise the 1947 "Journey of Reconciliation" in 1961, this time to be called the "Freedom Ride." On May 4, thirteen activists—seven blacks, including Farmer and John Lewis of SNCC, and six whites, including Peck and Albert Bigelow—departed on a Trailways bus from Washington, D.C., in a desegregated seating arrangement. Jim Peck was the only Freedom Rider who had participated in the Journey of Reconciliation.

Throughout Virginia and North Carolina, the group asserted itself as a desegregated cadre on buses, in terminals, and at lunch counters without serious incident. The first violent confrontation took place in South Carolina, where Lewis and

Bigelow were beaten by a white mob. This was but a foretaste, however, of what awaited them farther along the road.

Despite warnings from the local black leader Fred Shuttlesworth that further violence awaited them in Alabama, the group continued on their prearranged itinerary, traveling on two buses toward Birmingham. The violence Shuttlesworth had feared met the riders at the Greyhound bus station in Anniston, Alabama. There, the Freedom Riders were confronted by a mob of over two hundred whites. One bus managed to pull out of the station after having all its windows broken, the driver not realizing that the tires had also been slashed. The driver managed to drive only six miles out of Anniston before he had to pull the bus off the road, where it was quickly surrounded by a portion of the mob that had followed in a convoy of cars. An incendiary bomb was hurled into the bus, gutting the interior with fire and forcing the Freedom Riders out to face their pursuers. Local police standing by refused to intervene. The situation would no doubt have rapidly worsened had not a group of cars presciently dispatched by Shuttlesworth arrived to rescue the besieged riders.

Meanwhile, before the second bus could leave the terminal, it was boarded by several men who severely beat Peck and fellow-rider Walter Bergman, a retired school administrator participating in the Freedom Ride with his wife. The driver of this second bus finally managed to drive from Anniston to the Birmingham station, where another dangerous mob awaited the group. Peck again took the brunt of this assault; he was beaten senseless with metal pipes and required fifty stitches. When no drivers could be found who were willing to drive the groups farther, CORE canceled the remainder of the Freedom Ride. Yet even in their attempt to call off their plans the group of riders was hampered by segregationists. They were delayed for several hours at the airport when bomb threats were phoned in against the plane they were waiting to take to New York. The group eventually did arrive in New York City, where Peck joined a picket line—on the same day he had been beaten.

At this point, the close ties CORE had forged with the

Diane
Nash

student movement during the sit-ins of the previous year proved their mettle. Angry that CORE had been forced to abandon the ride, John Lewis and other SNCC members in Nashville courageously decided to continue the Freedom Riders' itinerary. After being turned away by Birmingham police, the SNCC group returned in greater numbers and eventually succeeded in continuing the Freedom Ride from Birmingham to Montgomery. They were so brutally attacked by a mob in Montgomery, however, that the Kennedy administration was finally embarrassed into sending six hundred federal marshals to protect the riders. At this point, King flew to Montgomery to participate in the reactivated ride. James Farmer (who had left the earlier incarnation of the Freedom Ride before the buses arrived in Anniston to attend his father's funeral) also flew down to Montgomery to reassert CORE's presence in the action. A coalition of CORE, SNCC, and SCLC then continued the Freedom Ride to Jackson, Mississippi. In Jackson, harassment arrests by local police led the protesters to initiate a policy of filling up the city's jails. Joined by hundreds of people, mostly students, who arrived in Jackson to be arrested, this tactic succeeded in keeping a national spotlight on the action throughout the summer and finally led to decisive federal action that enforced desegregated seating on interstate travel, the goal of the Journey of Reconciliation fourteen years before.[46]

The Freedom Rides kept the momentum begun by the sit-ins moving forward, adding a greater sense of urgency to the Civil Rights agenda. The rides catapulted CORE into national prominence on a par with SCLC and SNCC, leading to a dramatic increase in membership. The rides also cemented CORE's close links with the militant leaders of SNCC, links that would keep CORE on the cutting edge of black militancy, but a militancy that would splinter the organization with the emergence of black power.

The black freedom struggles of the early 1960s captured far more national attention than did the antinuclear activities of pacifists during the same period. Nonetheless, the antinuclear actions of the early 1960s continued to build important links between radical pacifists and white student activists around an antiwar agenda. In these years, Brad Lyttle remained an important organizer.

Sitting in a coffeeshop after the Polaris Action had crested, Lyttle and a few others decided to initiate a walk from San Francisco to Washington, D.C., and then across Europe to Moscow, to protest the nuclear arms race. In 1961, Lyttle led this first transcontinental peace walk in American history, a tiny knot of marchers (only about forty people when the group briefly swelled after passing by Chicago) who straggled their way across the nation, speaking in towns along their route. In Washington, Arthur Schlesinger, Jr., politely but stiffly met them on behalf of the Kennedy administration. They traveled to England (where they participated in a joint rally with Bertrand Russell's Committee for Nuclear Disarmament) and then walked across Belgium and both Germanys into Russia (where Muste had flown to negotiate their entry). The marchers were welcomed warmly by the Soviet Peace Committee and even allowed to stage a rally in Red Square bearing signs with their own choice of words, because Khrushchev hoped to use the marchers in his propaganda campaign to convince the world that the Soviet Union was an open society. (The marchers, though, were shifted from a meeting with Khrushchev to a meeting with his wife when they refused to support the Soviet "peace" position that effectively portrayed the United States as the principal aggressor.)

The San Francisco to Moscow Walk took about eighteen months in 1961 and 1962. Lyttle followed it up almost immediately with a Quebec to Guantanamo Walk, in 1963. While both walks enjoyed some media attention, however, they were far less effective at challenging the national conscience than the black freedom struggles of the same years. This was tacitly acknowledged by the marchers themselves when they diverted their march en route to Cuba to participate in the SNCC-led attempt to fill up the jails in Albany, Georgia. Even the pages of *Liberation* devoted far more attention to desegregation struggles in the South than to the peace marchers in 1962 and 1963. Indeed, many of the Quebec to Guantanamo marchers themselves seemed more interested in their Albany prison experience than in the other stages of their 1963 peace march.[47] Clearly, radical pacifists looked to the black movement for the nonviolent revolution for which they yearned in the early 1960s.

After the Quebec to Guantanamo Walk, which followed on the heels of the Omaha, Polaris, and San Francisco to Moscow actions, Brad Lyttle felt that he was emotionally exhausted. "I was unable to organize any major pacifist field projects after these," he recalls.[48]

Meanwhile, in 1963, the Civil Rights phase of the black freedom struggles reached perhaps its high-water mark when Randolph's dream of a March on Washington finally came to fruition. Rather than ten thousand blacks marching on the capital, as Randolph had envisioned in 1941, more than 250,000 people took part in August of 1963, making it the largest protest rally in American history up to that point. Bayard Rustin was given the primary responsibility for organizing the march, working as deputy director of the march committee under the nominal directorship of the venerable but aging Randolph. Again, Rustin's past Youth Communist ties and homosexuality plagued him, leading planners to make Randolph the titular head of the committee in case opponents tried to discredit the rally by launching a character assassination of Rustin.

Rustin did a superb organizational job, planning the welter of logistics and ensuring widespread media coverage of the event. Determined to keep the event as mainstream as possible, he played a key role in pressuring SNCC leader John Lewis to excise passages of his speech that were critical of the Kennedy administration. King, too, struck a cautious note in his speech, which may be one reason why the first half of the famous "I Have a Dream" speech was so flat. King only hit his stride in that address when he shifted away from his prepared notes to soar into poetical eschatology in the best Baptist preaching tradition, but that second half alone was so inspiring as to enshrine the speech as an American icon—and contribute enormously to King's apotheosis.

By 1963, the Left had experienced a remarkable resurgence after its nadir in the mid-1950s. At least one movement of the Left, the Civil Rights component of the black freedom struggles, could now call upon masses of people to participate in its protests. In this movement, radical pacifists who had been active since World War II played critical roles. Glenn Smiley and Bayard Rustin, through their influence on King, helped establish nonviolent direct action as the orthodox Civil Rights methodology. With the March on Washington, Rustin synthesized his radical pacifist experience with Randolph's mass action techniques in a powerful alchemy that pricked the conscience of the American people. CORE, too, in its reprise as a militant vanguard, helped shift the center of the Civil Rights movement further in a radical, direct action course.

Much had happened in the late 1950s and early 1960s on the antiwar front as well. SANE and CNVA had in complementary ways galvanized dissent against Cold War nuclear policies. CNVA and Dorothy Day's Catholic Worker had applied direct action tactics to their opposition to the military-industrial complex in creative ways and, in so doing, had developed important links with a new generation of student activists. Muste had done much to further these links by his efforts to foster dialogue and build coalitions on the Left. Most influential in this regard were his founding of *Liberation* and his support of Brad Lyttle and of nonexclusion, all of which kept the older radical pacifists fresh in the eyes of many younger radicals. In 1963, it appeared that the black freedom struggles would continue to absorb most of the attention of the Left. But events in Southeast Asia would soon become the focus of American protest. As antiwar sentiment became a groundswell in the mid-1960s, the peace efforts that radical pacifists had engaged in during the late 1950s and early 1960s would place them at the organizational center of the emerging antiwar coalitions.

Six

THE VIETNAM ERA

THE NEW RADICALISM

The New Radicalism is pluralistic, amorphous, and multilay-ered. Its three political strands—anarchism, pacifism, and social-ism—mingle in different proportions. . . . At its surface, political level, the New Radicalism is an anti-Establishment protest against all the obvious inequities of American life. It says that Negroes should vote, that America should follow a peaceful, noninterventionist foreign policy. . . . It is a series of individual criticisms many liberals can agree with. . . . At its second, more complex level, this movement is a moral revulsion against a soci-ety that is becoming increasingly corrupt. . . . Feeling this ethi-cal vacuum in the country, the New Radicals have made moral-ity and truth the touchstones of their movement. Like Gandhi, they try to "speak truth to power." Their politics are not particu-larly concerned with power or success, but rather with absolute moral alternatives like love, justice, equality, and freedom. Prac-tical, programmatic goals are of little interest. . . . At its third, subterranean level, the New Radicalism is an existential revolt against remote, impersonal machines that are not responsive to human needs. The New Radicals feel sharply the growing totalitarianism of life in this technological, urban decade. . . . From their fury at arbitrary power wielded by impersonal machines (governments, college administrations, welfare bureaucracies, draft boards, television networks) come some of the New Radicals' most innovative ideas. Participatory democracy—the notion that ordinary people should be able to affect all the decisions that control their lives. . . . It is its brilliant insight into the creeping authoritarianism of modern technology and bureaucracy that gives the New Radicalism its definitive qualities of decentralism, communitarianism, and existential humanism. Historically, the New Radicals' forebearers are the Whitman-Emerson-Thoreau transcendentalists, and the Joe Hill–Bill Hayward Wobblies.[1]

The above statement was not written to describe radical pacifism in the 1940s or 1950s but, rather, was written by Jack Newfield in 1966 to describe the student New Left identified most readily with SDS. This resemblance arises from the central role radical pacifism played in forging the underlying ethos of the new radical culture in the early- to mid-1960s.

The spirit of creative experimentalism that marked radical pacifism from its inception in the 1940s led it to develop a protest style more attuned to the tenor of the times than groups that had remained in one way or another shackled to organizations and concerns of the Old Left. Historian Penina M. Glazer, who has argued that the 1940s was a "decade of transition" in which the radicalism of the 1960s had its origins, posits that the groups most willing to experiment during this period were the groups that eventually exerted most influence on subsequent protest movements. In this regard, she concludes that "the radical pacifists were particularly dynamic."[2]

Centrally concerned with reasserting an autonomous self in modern life, radical pacifists rejected the Old Left from the start for its authoritarian tendencies. Freed from the organizational assumptions that still held other radical organizations of the Old Left enthralled, radical pacifists were the first group on the American Left in the 1940s to shift their agenda from labor to posit race and militarism as the key social issues of the day; to build an organizational structure that was decentralized and emphasized participatory democracy while questioning the necessity of strong leadership; that focused tactically on nonviolent civil disobedience as its primary methodology; and that developed a movement ethos that called for total lifestyle commitment and emphasized action over analysis, especially glorifying those such as Corbett Bishop and Jim Peck who "put their body upon the line."

The student leaders of the New Left were certainly influenced by people and movements other than radical pacifism—notably, European existentialists, such as Camus and Sartre, and American thinkers associated with *Politics* magazine, such as C. Wright Mills and David Riesman (all of whom had influenced radical pacifists as well). Yet the genealogy of radical pacifist influence upon the protest ethos of the emergent new radicalism of the 1960s is clear: Dwight Macdonald's essays on the centrality of individual moral sensibility that appeared in *Politics* during the mid-1940s, when he was deeply influenced by, and identified with, the radical pacifist movement; the role of CORE in establishing small-group direct action as a paradigmatic tactic for protest against segregation and the subsequent close association the student leaders of the sit-in movement and SNCC had with CORE, still under the leadership of Farmer and Peck; the influence Glenn Smiley, Bayard Rustin, and other radical pacifists had on the protest tactics adopted by King and the SCLC; the CNVA protests such as the Golden Rule and Brad Lyttle's actions as well as the Catholic Worker's civil defense protests, which attracted young white militants; Ken Calkins's Student Peace Union, which brought CNVA's methods to campus peace efforts; Muste's role in reaching out to young activists through his coalition work and his founding of *Liberation;* and the central role played by radical pacifists in the protests against American intervention in Vietnam are just the more salient means by which radical pacifists played a central role in shaping the ethos of postwar radicalism. Student activists of the early 1960s such as the founders of SDS assimilated much of this ethos from divergent sources on the Left, often unaware these influences had World War II C.O. pedigrees.

There was, however, a dark side to this radical pacifist influence upon the student activism of the 1960s. By reacting against the excesses of the Old Left, radical pacifists embraced a structure and program that were well suited to small groups crying out in the political wilderness of the 1940s and early 1950s but were not particularly suited to movements with a mass base. Decentralized organizations that embraced nonhierarchical, participatory methods and nonexclusion were vulnerable to takeover from within by disciplined, insurgent fringe groups. The primacy of action over analysis in radical pacifist culture had been a breath of fresh air on the Left in the 1950s after so many years of the stale, paralyzing scholasticism of the Old Left. The radical pacifist penchant for cathartic symbolic protest proved a powerful method for nonviolently facing down oppressive institutions, such as segregation in the South, in a way that captured media attention. With CNVA, however, this emphasis took on added degrees of impatience and bravado, marked by a glorification of placing one's body at risk, such as swimming aboard a disembarking nuclear attack submarine, to demonstrate the depth of one's convictions. Such methods often necessitated a continual increase in the militancy—or at least novelty—of actions in order to keep the public's limited attention focused on the protests. This proclivity, that lies in the very nature of symbolic protest in an age of mass media, privileged the most militant Jacobins who periodically arose within organizations of the new radicalism throughout the 1950s and 1960s. In the hands of groups such as SDS, which lacked the discipline of Gandhist underpinnings, the tendency toward expressionist activism eventually eclipsed the more instrumentalist task of building sustainable movements altogether by the late 1960s. Reflecting back on the 1960s, Paul Booth, former president of SDS, recalls: "We didn't start out with very good ideas about strategy, in part because the pacifist-direct action people who influenced us weren't into strategy. . . . Unfortunately, the Old Left didn't influence us: we viewed them as intellectually bankrupt. But they were the only people in the society who knew what . . . a mass organization was or how you worked in one."[3] While the radical pacifist ethos of putting one's body upon the line that infused dissent in the late 1950s and 1960s would generate some of the most poignant and searing images of creative protest in American history, the privileging of such action at the expense of analysis would result in a Left remarkably devoid of intellectual content after the collapse of its activist momentum in 1969. As late as 1963, however, no one would have predicted that the denouement of the history of radical pacifism—and of the postwar Left in general—would take place over the issue of United States intervention in Vietnam.

RESISTANCE TO THE VIETNAM WAR

Protest against U.S. intervention in Vietnam was a lonely affair in the early 1960s. Prior to 1963, the Vietnam conflict, when it was mentioned at all at peace demonstrations, was subsumed in a list of grievances. The first demonstration solely on the issue of Vietnam took place in 1963 when two young Catholic Workers, Tom Cornell and Christopher Sanders Kearns, held a vigil for nine days in front of the home of South Vietnam's observer at the United Nations. Dave McReynolds of the WRL arranged for about 250 of the regular New York activists, including Muste, to turn out for the tenth and last day of the protest. This was a sizable turnout for radical pacifism in the early 1960s. Cornell recalls that "we never had a demonstration of more than 250 people until the war got going."[4]

Gradually in 1964 Vietnam began to play a more important role in the thinking of radical pacifist activists, but in this they were almost alone on the Left. The Johnson administration was hardening its commitment to the South Vietnamese government, and the number of American advisors there was climbing. But the involvement of the United States in Vietnam was still far short of what could be termed war, and the news about America's growing commitment there was tucked away in the back pages of newspapers. SDS, two years old in 1964 and just beginning to emerge as the most influential student group in the country, was engrossed with its own Economic Research and Action Project (ERAP), whereby white college students were sent into ghettoes to organize community action for better living and working conditions. The results were less than spectacular, but SDS remained committed to the idea and largely oblivious to events in Southeast Asia throughout 1964.

On July 3, 1964, radical pacifists held a demonstration against the American escalation in Vietnam just outside the White House gates. Protesters included such stalwarts as Muste and Dellinger as well as some fresh faces in the antiwar camp, Joan Baez and the brothers Daniel and Philip Berrigan. The Berrigans were Catholic priests who were on the small progressive wing of the Catholic Church in America that included the Catholic Worker and Thomas Merton.

At the La Guardia airport that morning, a telling interchange occurred. Dave Dellinger bumped into Bayard Rustin, who, by coincidence, was traveling to the White House to participate in the ceremony for the signing of the 1964 Civil Rights Act that same day. Rustin had sat in on the planning meetings for the antiwar demonstration, in which a statement against the escalation in Vietnam had been drafted. Rustin, however, had been unwilling to sign the statement. Sitting on the flight to Washington together, Dellinger tried to persuade Rustin to stop by the peace rally on his way from the White House to sign the antiwar statement with one of the pens passed out at the signing of the landmark Civil Rights legislation. Significantly, Rustin refused to combine the two issues. "That was the point when I knew he'd gone over the hill," Dellinger remembers.[5]

This exchange was a clear indication of the deepening rift between Rustin and radical pacifists. In the early- to mid-1960s, Rustin increasingly opposed an alliance between the leadership of the black freedom struggles and his former radical pacifist cohorts. Rustin repeatedly and strenuously advised King against taking a public stand in opposition to the Vietnam War, arguing that it would be detrimental to King's leadership of black America to take a stand on controversial issues outside the direct concern of Civil Rights struggles. Increasingly associating himself with Randolph, Rustin felt that the most useful allies for Civil Rights leaders were to be found in labor unions and the liberal establishment. Such an approach obviously precluded overt criticism of American policy in Vietnam, which was being directed by a Democratic president and was supported by most mainstream labor groups.

In February 1965, Rustin gave full expression to his journey from radicalism to a cautious liberalism in an article entitled "From Protest to Politics."[6] In this article, Rustin argued that the protest methods of the black freedom struggles were beginning to reach the limits of their efficacy. Rustin called upon black leaders to pursue a new alignment with such mainstream liberal institutions as the labor movement (which did not have a stellar record on the issue of race) and the Democratic party in order to more effectively translate black America's discontent into concrete legislation and programs. Looking back on the past decade of black activism, Rustin concluded: "What began as a protest movement is being challenged to translate itself into a political movement." Failure to forge alliances with liberals, he warned, would relegate the Civil Rights movement to "majestic isolation, except for a tiny band of fervent white initiates." Rustin followed through on his ideas by becoming executive director of the A. Philip Randolph Institute, which worked closely with the AFL-CIO, and by urging black leaders to support— or at least stay silent about—Johnson's burgeoning war effort in Vietnam in order to keep the administration's momentum behind the War on Poverty. Rustin made many enemies throughout the Left when he urged the Mississippi Freedom Democratic party to accept Johnson's token compromise at the Democratic convention in 1964 and when he tried to prevent a march against the Vietnam War sponsored by SDS in 1965.

Rustin's convictions that street protest against racial discrimination was coming up against its own limitations and that the progressive Left and the liberal establishment needed each other have in certain respects proved remarkably prescient. Yet Rustin's shift to the center, occurring at precisely the time when most activists felt that direct action was proving to be a powerful method for social transformation, and when they increasingly viewed the Johnson administration's policy in Southeast Asia as blatantly immoral, left radical pacifists aghast. Staughton Lynd, whose work as director of the Freedom Schools sponsored by SNCC in Mississippi during the "Freedom Summer" of 1964[7] had left him in no mood to soften his criticisms of the Johnson administration, wrote a scathing condemnation of Rustin's new positions in *Liberation,* a magazine on whose editorial board Rustin and Lynd both still sat. Lynd pulled few punches in his article, "Coalition Politics or Nonviolent Revolution?" stating: "Rustin has permitted himself to drift into that posture which once evoked epithets such as 'labor lieutenant of capitalism.'"[8] Lynd's anger arose in part from personal feelings of betrayal. "I singled out Bayard . . . ," he later wrote, "most of all because Bayard Rustin has for so long inspired myself and others of my generation as a passionate practitioner of radical civil disobedience and nonviolent revolution."[9]

Lynd's strident condemnation of Rustin unleashed a storm of debate on the Left. Lynd was taken to task in a letter to *Liberation*'s editors signed by, among others, Michael Harrington, Irving Howe, Norman Thomas, and radical pacifists Mulford Sibley and George Willoughby. These signatories characterized Lynd's article as a "character assassination" that "does not belong on the democratic Left." Lynd, they wrote, "resorts to language which he may consider natural to the 'new Left' but which strikes us as a dismal echo from the old and discredited Left."[10] The editors of *Liberation,* who had encouraged Lynd's criticisms, now, in turn, rose to his defense, declaring that they "never regarded Staughton Lynd's article as in any sense constituting 'character assassination' of Bayard Rustin. . . . Persons impressed by Staughton's courageous opposition to the Vietnam war might well question the appropriateness of what might be considered an organized attempt to brand Staughton Lynd as a 'character

Bayard Rustin. Photo Courtesy, Estate of Bayard Rustin.

assassin.'"[11] Rustin declined to publish a response to Lynd's criticism in *Liberation,* and he resigned from its editorial board in early 1966.

By the time of this exchange, Vietnam was arriving front and center in American politics. Vietnam had been thrust into greater domestic prominence after a Communist attack on United States troops at Pleiku in February of 1965. The Johnson administration seized upon the attack to pursue a dramatic escalation of American involvement in the Vietnam War. As domestic attention shifted to the tiny Asian nation few had much knowledge about, teach-ins were organized on college campuses across the country throughout the spring to educate the intellectual community about the war. Many at the teach-ins, especially a student body restive after the 1964 Freedom Summer in Mississippi and the Free Speech Movement at Berkeley, found the administration's propositions for the necessity of such intervention unconvincing. The teach-ins, consequently, contributed to a groundswell of student pressure on SDS to take a stand against the war.

SDS leaders, however, hesitated to divert their focus to the war. Paul Potter, SDS president at the time, feared that Vietnam was a marginal and transitory issue that would distract the organization from its focus on the ERAP work in American ghettoes. Reluctantly, though, he agreed to sponsor a march against the war in Washington in April. Over twenty thousand people, mostly student age, participated in the SDS rally, where they were addressed by Potter, I. F. Stone, SNCC leader Robert Parris (formerly and subsequently Bob Moses), and Staughton Lynd, among others. The rally received widespread media attention, which convinced college students across the country for years to come that SDS was the chief organization expressing opposition to the Vietnam War. Ironically, however, hawkish criticism in the press convinced the leadership of SDS to back away from sponsoring further such rallies.

Meanwhile, radical pacifists were planning a demonstration

of their own in Washington for August of 1965. The size of the April demonstration organized by SDS had surprised everyone. Muste, Dellinger, and Lynd hoped to have a similar turnout for their demonstration, built on the broadest possible coalition of activist forces, including traditional and radical pacifists, unionists, black activists, and students. The ideological umbrella they hoped would unify such diverse interests was drawn from recent speeches Lynd had been giving that portrayed the government as unresponsive to democratic impulses. The war in Vietnam and the government's economic and racial policies, Lynd argued, were the creation of a bureaucracy that did not truly represent the interests of people at the grassroots level. Thus was born the Assembly of Unrepresented People, which began on the twentieth anniversary of the atomic bombing of Hiroshima and ended on the anniversary of Nagasaki's destruction. The turnout for the assembly did not match the SDS march, but radical pacifist organizers were nonetheless pleased to have from one to two thousand participants, of whom about 350 were arrested for committing civil disobedience at the Capitol building.

The assembly began with a silent vigil followed by a rally at the White House. The next day, the crowd dispersed to workshops on a wide array of issues and concerns. On the last day of the rally, protesters marched to the Capitol building, led by Lynd, Dellinger, and Bob Moses of SNCC. Along the route, counterdemonstrators splashed red paint on the three of them. The image the media carried of these three activists marching on the Capitol with red paint streaked over their faces and clothes resonated with Americans' ambivalent view of antiwar demonstrators: undaunted by criticism and assault but, in the popular mind, still smeared with suspicions of being "red."

The radical pacifist organizers were thrilled with the assembly, hoping that it betokened a new broad-based coalition. On the initiative of Jerry Rubin, who had made his mark as organizer of the Vietnam Day Committee in Berkeley, they optimistically formed the National Coordinating Committee to End the War in Vietnam (NCCEWVN) during the weekend. Radical pacifists at the time failed to fully appreciate the seriousness

Dave Dellinger, Staughton Lynd, and Robert Parris Moses leading the Assembly of Unrepresented People while spattered with red paint, Washington,
D.C., August 1965. Photo by Neil Haworth, reprinted with permission from
the War Resisters League files.

of the rifts on the Left that would make a multi-issue umbrella
organization so difficult to maintain in the 1960s: there was
great tension over the primacy of race among activists and SDS
persisted in backing away from any protest against the Vietnam
War since its April demonstration. Yet the radical pacifists' faith
in the efficacy of coalition building would make NCCEWVN
the forerunner of more successful such organizations—at the
helm of which Muste and Dellinger would soon be regularly
calling tens of thousands of people into the streets to demonstrate against the escalating war in Southeast Asia.

In 1966, Lynd took a daring step when he traveled to Hanoi
with Tom Hayden of SDS and Herbert Aptheker, a Marxist historian. Lynd, who had been reared in the upper echelons of

academia, was then a prominent historian of colonial America struggling to balance his activism with his role as a member of Yale's history department. Shortly after his return to the United States, however, Yale denied him tenure.

Trips to Vietnam would become somewhat popular on the Left. Dellinger made such a junket later in 1966. A month before his death in 1967, Muste traveled to Vietnam with Barbara Deming and representatives from Women Strike for Peace. While visiting Saigon, Muste and Deming engaged in civil disobedience to protest the policies of the South Vietnamese government. Deming recalls being concerned about Muste's health at one point on the hot day when they were arrested. Just then, Muste looked across at her, smiled, and exclaimed, "It's a good life!" [12] In 1968, it would be the turn of Howard Zinn and Dan Berrigan. And many other antiwar activists would make the trip in subsequent years, although doing so had lost some of its controversiality by the 1970s. In part, such trips were viewed as a means to personally convey opposition to the United States government's execution of the war in a way that was sure to stir controversy. Such trips also stemmed for some participants from a tendency on the Left to romanticize armed Third World revolutionaries—a weakness, oddly, that some radical pacifists shared at the time.

In early 1967, Muste and Dellinger were again hard at work organizing a broad-based coalition. Originally initiated by students who wanted to demonstrate the growing strength of the antiwar movement by holding a protest with perhaps tens of thousands of marchers, the ad hoc Spring Mobilization to End the War in Vietnam far exceeded the modest goals of its planners. As the scale of the planning grew, primary responsibility for organizing the rally moved from the students who had envisioned it to the experienced hands of Muste, Dellinger, and Sidney Peck, a professor at Case Western Reserve University who had been involved in the teach-in movement.

At the same time, SDS, despite the hesitations of its leadership, was beginning to show a new willingness to focus on the Vietnam War. There were many factors contributing to this.

There was, of course, the rapid escalation of the war itself. By 1967, American troop commitment in Vietnam was at nearly 400,000—and growing. Few issues were more pressing in the minds of the male rank and file within SDS than that of the draft. SDS realized just in time that the New Left would pass it by if it did not lead its members on the issue of Vietnam.

SDS was also driven into the antiwar camp in 1967 by the emergence of the black power movement. First arising within SNCC (and associated with Stokely Carmichael), black power swept across the spectrum of black militancy in 1966. Undoubtedly its most visceral organizational symbol was the gun-toting Black Panther party. "Black power" was nowhere clearly defined, but it generally denoted a move in the black community toward black-led institutions. This shift caught white activists by surprise.

Closely allied with SNCC since the sit-in movement, Farmer, joined by black activists Floyd McKissick and Roy Innis, quickly followed SNCC's lead by heading CORE in a black power direction in 1966. CORE's twenty-third annual convention in July of 1966 was marked by militant rhetorical flourishes, and at the 1967 convention the word "multiracial" was voted out of the organization's constitution.[13]

CORE's black power stance led to an exodus of white liberal support that would seriously undermine the organization's membership—not to mention its financial—base. Author Lillian Smith, the Georgia native who had written *Strange Fruit* and other books challenging racial discrimination and had been an active member of CORE since the late 1940s, resigned from the organization immediately after the 1966 convention. "CORE has been infiltrated by . . . nihilists, black nationalists, and plain old-fashioned haters, who have finally taken over," she lamented.[14]

Although CORE never officially barred whites from the organization, Jim Peck was unmistakably squeezed out. A loophole in the organization's rules protected Peck from being fired as editor of the group's newsletter, the *COREelator,* a post he had held since 1948. CORE's leadership got around this by simply abolishing the *COREelator*. Dave McReynolds believes that Peck was forced out of CORE in a "terribly undignified way." Peck, he thinks, was "never intellectually able to understand why it was necessary" for the movement to expel whites.[15] Bill Sutherland recalls that Peck was "very bitter," feeling that "people like Farmer had betrayed him and betrayed the ideal of CORE."[16] Peck wrote an angry—and, at times, plaintive—essay in the October 1966 issue of *Liberation*. "I worked for CORE, without remuneration," he wrote, "from the initial freedom ride (Journey of Reconciliation) in 1947 until 1965 when I was ousted because of my skin color." He reminded readers that "I was beaten almost to death on the first of the 1961 Freedom Rides," and he concluded, "Why can't we end this period of . . . dissension in the Movement and resume nonviolent action in the streets, singing 'We Shall Overcome'—and without deleting the stanza 'Black and white together'?"[17]

Black power advocates cast SDS members out of the militant wing of the black freedom struggle as well. Many in SDS had participated with SNCC in Freedom Summer and other activities in the deep South, but these white activists now found almost as much hostility to their continued participation from black activists as they did from white segregationists. SDS's ERAP workers also found blacks in the urban ghettoes less hospitable to white college students who came in with visions of leading them to the political Promised Land. Precluded from further action on the race and urban fronts, SDS leaders moved back to the issue of Vietnam in 1967. Ironically, many college students who looked to SDS for leadership in the antiwar movement never knew that SDS had moved away from the issue after the April 1966 protest in Washington.

When SDS did resolve to embrace the Vietnam War as its focal point in 1967, new student leaders within the organization brought a frenzied edge to their war resistance that grew from an amalgam of mounting anger about the war, drug-induced unreality, and emulation of the Black Panthers' "in-your-face" belligerence that teetered dangerously at the edge of romanticizing violence. These tendencies within SDS would present themselves most clearly when Bay Area students engaged police in street battles as part of an attempt to shut down the Oakland induction center in October of 1967. Radical pacifists looked to a coalition with these younger radicals. Muste, Dellinger, and Lynd publicly supported much of the new militancy, although they persistently urged adherence to nonviolent methods for social change. Lynd, for instance, expressed strong empathy for black power advocates in a 1966 *Liberation* article, where he compared the new slogan favorably to the thinking of DuBois. But he closed with a cautionary reminder that DuBois "continued to advocate nonviolence."[18] As the student antiwar movement shifted from protest against the war to active attempts on the domestic front to disrupt the government's ability to wage the war, Lynd quickly supported and encouraged the confrontational tactics. Lynd, for instance, in an article in *Liberation* entitled "Resistance: From Mood to Strategy," commented favorably that, "as usual, Berkeley points a direction in its week-long attempt to obstruct the functioning of the Oakland Induction Center."[19]

Dellinger particularly among radical pacifists sought to build an alliance with this new student activism and attempted to steer it into broader coalitions. Dellinger's rhetoric during these years appeared intemperate to some pacifists. Dave McReynolds considers Dellinger "a person to be arrested with," because of Dellinger's personal warmth, yet McReynolds always tried to avoid speaking before Dellinger at a protest, because, he says, Dellinger, "has to position himself to the Left of you." Dellinger, McReynolds sums up, was "correct twice a day, like a broken clock."[20] Ira Sandperl feels that Dellinger "wants to be seen as 'in' all the time" and that Dellinger and Muste "loved the huge number of marvellous young kids that were gathering under their feet." Sandperl believes that Muste and Dellinger "became very shy about speaking about nonviolence" once "they got a movement going," and he even asserts that Dellinger "went back on his pacifist position . . . in the sixties."[21] Dellinger, however, maintains that he "never changed basically from being totally committed to nonviolence."[22]

While in retrospect the rhetoric of Dellinger (and, to be sure, many others on the Left) in the late 1960s sometimes appears overblown, unconsidered, and even occasionally affected, this was nonetheless the lexicon of their milieu—at a moment that was easily misperceived as revolutionary. By positioning himself further leftward than some other pacifists, Dellinger certainly remained consistent with his lifelong rebel stance, and he proved effective at reaching out to the new batch of student leaders. It must also be borne in mind that, prior to 1968, the irrationalism and violence that inhered in student rebellion had not fully surfaced. After the Chicago debacle, Dellinger would cast a more critical eye on the student-led New Left and counterculture.

On February 10, 1967, the antiwar movement lost its most venerable leader when A. J. Muste died at the age of eighty-two—true to form, less than a month after his trip to Vietnam. The mantle of leadership of the pacifist wing in the antiwar movement was now fully assumed by Dave Dellinger, who plunged into preparations for the Spring Mobilization to End the War in Vietnam (Spring Mobe).

Realizing the logistical difficulty of getting a bicoastal movement to converge in one large demonstration but determined to demonstrate the mass base that the antiwar movement had gained, organizers decided to hold simultaneous rallies in New York and San Francisco on April 15. The scale of the turnout exceeded all expectations. More than fifty thousand people marched in San Francisco. Estimates of the crowd in New York City ranged from 200,000 to half a million, with groups ranging from SANE to SNCC represented.

Against the strong opposition of some of his closest advisers, including Rustin and New York lawyer Stanley Levison, Martin Luther King spoke against the war at the Spring Mobe rally. King had been playing Hamlet over the issue of the war for more than a year. King himself appears to have felt that the Vietnam War was a mistaken and morally suspect venture, but he was under enormous pressure from both sides. On the one hand, he was held back in part by Rustin and others in the black movement who felt that he should steer clear of the war issue. On the other hand, King felt pressured by militants in SNCC who had come out forcefully against the war in 1966. Finally, on April 4, King made his first public commitment to the antiwar movement in a speech at New York City's Riverside Church. Meanwhile, he agreed to participate in the Spring Mobilization of April 15. Yet still he equivocated. When King learned that the program also included Stokely Carmichael of SNCC, who had alienated King with his Black Power slogan during their joint march through Mississippi the previous year, King reconsidered his participation in the rally. Long meetings ensued over this and subsequent concerns expressed by King and his aides. Dellinger believes that a turning point occurred when he spelled out to Andy Young, close aide to King, that the rally was sizing up to be the largest antiwar demonstration to date. King, Dellinger told Young, "is long overdue on this question and if he fails to act now history will pass him by and from now on his influence will be minimized."[23] King, in the end, did participate in the Spring Mobilization on the same program as Carmichael. After his speech, he commented to Dellinger that the rally was "greater than the '63 civil rights rally" (the March on Washington).[24]

Due to his stature as a Civil Rights leader, King had to withstand a torrent of public excoriation for his identification with the antiwar movement, including harsh condemnation by Ralph Bunche, another African-American winner of the Nobel Peace Prize. His decision to participate also meant a shift in King's inner circle. Rustin would never again have King's ear as he had in the late 1950s and early 1960s.

Thrilled by the April 15 demonstrations, Dellinger converted what had been an ad hoc Spring Mobilization Committee into a permanent organization, the Mobilization Committee to End the War in Vietnam (Mobe). At the same time, he initiated a series of planning discussions that led to a call for a national demonstration in Washington for October of 1967. Again, the radical pacifist leadership placed considerable emphasis on making the demonstration as broadly representative of antiwar forces as possible, an emphasis that was key to ensuring a sizable turnout. To help the Mobe organize the all-important student faction, Dellinger recruited Jerry Rubin to join the planning committee. Rubin had proven an able organizer in the Bay area. To Dellinger's surprise, however, Rubin had undergone a transformation since Dellinger and Lynd had last seen him at the Vietnam Day rally Rubin organized at Berkeley.

In concert with Abbie Hoffman, Rubin had founded a new subgroup within the student Left: the Yippies. Rubin and Hoffman visualized the Yippies as a synthesis of hippie counterculture with the radical politics of the New Left. Never more than a handful of adherents, the Yippies were able to capture considerable media attention with their outrageous antics, usually symbolic clowning with political overtones that provided ready-to-order sound bytes for the media. The consequent attention paid to the Yippies made them appear far more numerous and influential than they were. This style of media-oriented symbolic protest by a handful of creative activists was similar in certain respects to the tactics used by small groups of radical pacifists in the 1940s and 1950s, yet the Yippies added a dangerous layer of irrationalism.

The Mobe's original plan had been to begin the October demonstration with a rally at the Lincoln Memorial, followed by a march to the Pentagon, where those who chose to would participate in civil disobedience. This agenda tried to provide for an array of participants with various forms of protest. After Rubin's arrival at the Mobe office, a levitation of the Pentagon and an exorcism of the building's evil spirits were added to the agenda.

As the antiwar movement built steam, it became more fractious. Even within radical pacifism, which had largely avoided the major schisms that marked the Old Left, new fault lines became evident. Dave McReynolds resigned from *Liberation* in June of 1967, charging that Dellinger was too domineering and was losing his pacifist moorings. Doubtless, Muste would have been able to hold the editorial staff together if he had been alive.

Yet the October demonstration in Washington managed in

many ways to accommodate—even to celebrate—the diversity of the antiwar coalition that had coalesced in 1967, with protest ranging from quiet witness to disciplined civil disobedience to Yippie hijinks. Over 100,000 people gathered at the Lincoln Memorial on October 21 to hear a long series of speeches by William Sloane Coffin, John Lewis of SNCC, and Dellinger, as well as the political folk music of Phil Ochs. In the early afternoon, Dellinger commenced the march to the Pentagon, warning the crowd that illegal civil disobedience would take place there. The slogan the organizers had adopted for the rally was "From Protest to Resistance," capturing the increasingly confrontative mood of the movement as well as posing a counterpoint to Rustin's article, "From Protest to Politics."[25] Now, organizers hoped to bring massive resistance to the steps of the Pentagon itself.

Over fifty thousand people joined in the march across Washington to the Pentagon, under the careful watch of both the military and the media. The organizers had a permit for a peaceful protest outside the building. Shortly after arriving there, however, Dave Dellinger and Brad Lyttle led a small group that included Noam Chomsky in committing civil disobedience by entering an area that was outside the permit's specifications.

The decision by Dellinger and Lyttle to commit civil disobedience left the crowd in an awkward position after the only clear leaders of the rally had been hauled away. No one appears to have given clear thought to what the demonstrators would do at the Pentagon. Some student radicals cursed the soldiers and threw things at them, but they were quickly caught, beaten, and arrested. This was one of the first times that a national audience had seen such "trashing" tactics, and middle America was not amused. A number of Yippies engaged in their new "flower power" tactics, which also challenged the sensibilities of the American public. The most lasting and poignant image to come from the Pentagon action, though, was the photograph of a countercultural young man placing a flower in the barrel of a bayoneted gun held by a soldier of about the same age.

Sydney Peck tried to bring some order to the proceedings as dusk descended on the rally, but most people simply milled around. Gradually, much of the crowd drifted away. Several thousand did stay on the Pentagon steps through the night, ringed in by soldiers. Protesters tried, unsuccessfully, to get the soldiers to mutiny. In the morning, only a few hundred stalwarts persisted in the Pentagon vigil. Those who stayed on after the expiration of the permit were promptly carted off to new accommodations.

The critical reviews of the Pentagon Action were decidedly mixed. Many liberals and conservatives alike were horrified at the behavior of the more countercultural demonstrators. Dellinger, on the other hand, wrote enthusiastically that "a revolutionary elan" had "developed among the resisters" over the weekend, proving that a "creative synthesis of Gandhi and guerrilla" was "practical."[26] Dellinger saw in the predominantly peaceful and diverse action convincing evidence that broad-based coalitions such as the Mobe continued to prove their worth as the movement grew. "Without the massive numbers made possible by the presence of all these types . . . , the day would have had far less impact," he concluded.[27]

Growing numbers of activists in 1967 believed that they were living in a revolutionary moment. Only two years before, organizers for the Assembly of Unrepresented People had been pleased with a turnout that spilled over into four figures. The explosive growth of the movement fed a mistaken belief that revolution was imminent. This in turn encouraged increasingly incendiary rhetoric on the radical edge of activism, fostering a climate in which pacifists were often dismissed as political milquetoasts by student militants. Dellinger tried to appeal to student radicals with his proposed "synthesis of Gandhi and guerrilla," which he conceived as "a militant form of Gandhism" to be a "substitute" for violence.[28] Dellinger also admonished other activists that "we must not cut ourselves off from the millions who are just beginning to oppose the war, . . . who are prepared to dissent but not to rebel."[29] Yet even as mainstream America came to oppose the war in greater numbers, the increasingly violent tenor and style of the antiwar movement—especially the student wing of the movement—alienated many potential participants.

CHICAGO

1968 was among the most wrenching and disorienting years in America's history. For some time, the American military and political leadership had been assuring the public that the war in Vietnam was being won. Then, in late January, Communist forces mounted the Tet Offensive, a simultaneous assault on over thirty of the largest cities throughout South Vietnam. While the intention of the offensive remains unclear and while the military aftermath of the offensive left the Communist forces in the South exposed and vulnerable, the most important result of the Tet Offensive was its impact on the "credibility gap" between the Johnson administration and the American people. Tet convinced many Americans that the Vietnam War, whatever its morality, was unwinnable. When General Westmoreland, commander of American forces in Vietnam, asked for over 200,000 more troops in the aftermath of the Tet Offensive to supplement the half-million U.S. soldiers already there, the Johnson administration balked. At least part of the administration's consideration was its fear of the antiwar movement's potential to wreak domestic havoc if Westmoreland's request were met. Then came the final blow to Johnson's presidency. Senator Eugene McCarthy, an uninspiring candidate running for the Democratic party's presidential nomination on a peace platform, humiliated the incumbent by running about even with Johnson in the New Hampshire primary on March 12. On the last day of March, Johnson announced that he would not seek reelection.

Yet the shocks of 1968 were just getting underway. A few days after Johnson's surprise announcement, on April 4, Martin Luther King was felled by an assassin's bullet. Two months later, on June 6, Robert Kennedy was murdered while attending a celebration for his victory in the California Democratic primary.

Death, destruction, and unpredictable change hung like a sword of Damocles over 1968. Americans watching the nightly news were regularly updated by Walter Cronkite on the week's war casualties. From their living rooms, Americans watched youths influenced by Western counterculture briefly liberate Czechoslovakia, only to be crushed by Soviet tanks. And they saw students aligned with labor unions battle police in the streets of Paris.

Turmoil became normative on America's college campuses in 1968. In April, an SDS protest escalated into a student take-over of Columbia University. Columbia became a model for campus takeovers across the country. The subsequent brutality displayed by police while clearing Columbia's buildings after several days of standoff fed a disturbing and increasingly common belief among activists on the nation's campuses that it was a revolutionary activity to engage in petty provocation of the police.

On May 17, nine radical pacifists led by the Berrigan brothers destroyed draft files in Catonsville, Maryland, by burning them with napalm. This action, led by two Catholic priests, sent a jolt through America's Catholic community and was much analyzed in public discourse. What was perhaps most instructive about the action, however, was that such willful destruction of federal property, which would have rent CNVA asunder ten years before, seemed relatively tame in its nonviolent discipline compared to the action regularly taking place on the nation's streets and campuses in 1968.

Meanwhile, plans for a protest at the Democratic convention, slated for Chicago in August, were underway in the Mobe's headquarters. Dellinger and Tom Hayden were the key organizers. Under Dellinger's leadership, the Mobe had increasingly become a three-part organization representing radical pacifists, New Left student activists led by Hayden and Rennie Davis, and Yippies, led by Rubin and Hoffman. Dellinger managed to maintain some semblance of broad-based cohesion, but the cohesion was tenuous. As August approached, for instance, it became clear that the major groups within Mobe could not agree on protest rhetoric or tactics, so it was decided that each group would hold its own Chicago demonstration under the nominal aegis of the Mobe and with some loose coordination between the leadership. It was becoming painfully evident that the Left was fracturing beyond the ability to lead.

The shift in the makeup of the Mobe was evident in the new tone of *Liberation* which Dellinger effectively inherited after Muste's death. More countercultural articles appeared with titles such as "The Yippees Are Coming!" written by Marty Jezer (the most thoughtful of the group around Hoffman),[30] and "The Post-Competitive, Comparative Game of a Free City," written by the Diggers, the scions of Haight-Ashbury.[31]

As plans for a demonstration at the Democratic convention progressed through the summer, the rhetoric on both sides led many well-meaning moderates to steer far clear of what was coming to appear like a showdown at high noon. Mayor Daley made it clear that he intended to teach the protesters a lesson, while Hayden, Rubin, and Hoffman continued to give public pronouncements that did not appear designed to defuse the situation.

A foreboding sense of danger hung over the last days of preparation for the Chicago protest, which resulted in a much smaller turnout than organizers had planned. About five thousand demonstrators eventually made their way into Lincoln Park on the last weekend in August as the convention got underway a short distance and many billy clubs away. The demonstrators were met by nearly twenty thousand police and National Guard troops. The police showed a rabid contempt for the demonstrators, who did little to assuage such feelings.

Chicago's police soon made good on Daley's threats, as the bloodiest political convention in American history got underway. The troops assaulted protesters regardless of their behavior. Dellinger's pacifist contingent was beaten as they sat nonviolently just as savagely as the SDS people who engaged in mobile street battles. Journalists and television newspeople were beaten, as well, in what a subsequent government investigation termed a "police riot." Dellinger desperately exhorted the crowd to remain nonviolent, but few among the protesters heeded him. In the face of such repression, Hayden exhorted the crowd with angry rhetoric: "If they want blood to flow from our heads the blood will flow from a lot of other heads around this city and around the country."[32]

As the violence continued night after night in the streets of Chicago, television coverage of the Democratic convention gradually gave way to the war zone just outside the hall. On the evening that delegates were nominating Hubert Humphrey as the Democratic standard-bearer, images of events unfolding in the streets outside suddenly appeared on television monitors scattered about the convention floor, prompting Senator Ribicoff to excoriate Daley from the convention podium for using "Gestapo tactics" to quell dissent. At this, the convention exploded into disarray. America, it seemed, was coming apart, with the whole world watching, under the glare of television floodlights.

Dellinger's reaction to the convention was complex. On the one hand, he was outraged at the brutality of the police.[33] He even appeared to feel a certain exhilaration over the street battles with the police. Using heavily male-gendered language, he wrote in *Liberation* that "the triumph of Chicago was the triumph of street protesters who displayed courage, imagination, flexibility, and fraternal solidarity as they refused to knuckle under to the police. . . . There is a heady sense of manhood that comes from advancing from apathy to commitment, from timidity to courage, from passivity to aggressiveness. . . . There is an intoxication that comes from standing up to the police at last."[34] Such a statement veered perilously close to the rhetoric of those self-styled urban guerrillas in SDS who touted street violence. Dellinger, to be sure, believed that with proper, experienced leadership the younger generation of radicals could be led to dissent in ways that were more meaningful to the crisis of the times than calling police Nazis or trashing city streets. In order to provide this leadership in the milieu of the late 1960s, it may, indeed, have been necessary to prove adept at the game of revolutionary rhetoric. Never one to be outflanked on his left, Dellinger had always been multilingual in this regard, sounding remarkably Old Left when he felt this was the lexicon of his target audience.[35] Old Left rhetoric, after all, was what radicals of Dellinger's generation had cut their teeth on in the 1930s, and now knee-jerk confrontationalism with a revolutionary patina was decidedly hip.

On the balancing side, Dellinger chided many of his fellow pacifists for their timidity in choosing not to participate in the protest, where their experience might have leavened the proceedings with more discipline and content. "I wish," he wrote, "that there had been a greater turnout of people experienced in militant nonviolence—more, for example, who do not think it is revolutionary to taunt the police by screaming 'oink, oink' or 'pig' at them."[36]

The Chicago protest was a turning point for the antiwar movement. After the convention, the remnants of SDS spun off into new realms of irrationalism marked by a glorification of dadaistic violence, evident in 1969's puerile "Days of Rage." After the last convention of SDS in 1969, the splinter group, Weatherman, went underground to conduct a terrorist bombing campaign. And strange groups, such as Up Against the Wall, Motherfucker, began to wield some influence in radical circles.

Radical pacifists increasingly voiced their criticisms of these and other antiwar groups in 1969. In June, Staughton Lynd wrote in *Liberation* that he felt "sharply critical of present tendencies in national SDS" (although he added that "no one . . . wants to question the movement's historical commitment to non-exclusionism").[37] Later in the year, *Liberation* carried an article by a young student radical who took the new SDS leadership directly to task. Weatherman, wrote Carol McEldowney in the November issue, "is now the prime example of people into totally antagonistic politics which don't provide alternatives, which don't speak to people's needs . . . , which are based on hate that has slightly fascistic overtones." [38]

Increasingly, pacifists began to question the wisdom of maintaining the alliances with SDS and the Yippies Dellinger had forged. Antiwar sentiment was growing in middle America, where millions were coming to question the efficacy, if not the morality, of the Vietnam War. Many activists in 1969 and 1970 began to call for a return to traditional pacifist methods of non-violent protest—marches, speeches, and vigils—by which they hoped to lead the more moderate movement center.

THE CHICAGO TRIAL

In late March of 1969, Dellinger was indicted on charges of conspiracy along with Rubin, Hoffman, Hayden, and four other organizers of the Chicago protest, who became firmly fixed in the public imagination as the Chicago Seven (after the separation of Bobby Seale's defense from the rest), codefendants in the most celebrated and notorious trial of the decade. With the nation scrutinizing the trial of the antiwar movement's biggest celebrities, the Chicago Seven decided to attempt to turn the proceedings into an indictment of the Vietnam War. Judge Hoffman's iron-fisted style played into this tactic, for his repression of the defendants in the courtroom allowed them to more convincingly portray the trial as an authoritarian attempt to repress dissent against the war. To the surprise of no one who had followed the trial, the Chicago Seven were convicted. The convictions, however, were overturned in 1972.

Photographs from the trial show a striking dichotomy: Dellinger, in a suit and tie, looking stiff and uncomfortable alongside codefendants Hoffman and Rubin, dressed in hippy garb and engaging in prankish antics. Whether he willed it or no, Dellinger was finding that the youth leadership of the antiwar movement had shifted so far in the direction of the outrageous that his style of protest now spoke for moderate, even respectable, dissent. In 1952, Dellinger had looked to lifestyle as the key to revolutionary activity and had been critical of Muste's call for a fuller development of radical pacifism's discipline and ideological program. Ironically, in 1969 Dellinger found himself joining those who criticized the excesses of his ideological and stylistic heirs when he wrote: "Side by side with the creative insights [of the Yippies] are the ego-tripping, the fantasies and the bullshit—which in the end get in the way of making a revolution." Dellinger advocated more responsible dissent. "It is Yippie adventurism," he wrote, "to suggest there is any way of getting rid of repressive institutions without immense sacrifice, dedication and responsibility." [39]

NEW DIRECTIONS

For more than thirty-six blustery hours in November 1969 the March Against Death continued in an unbroken chain outside the White House. One by one, in peaceful and mournful protest, marchers in single file stopped to shout the name of an American soldier who had died in the Vietnam War, until all 45,000 had been accounted for. The morning after the March Against Death ended, more than half a million people filled downtown Washington in an overwhelmingly peaceful protest. The November demonstration had been largely organized by a new incarnation of the several Mobes, now called the New Mobilization Committee to End the War in Vietnam (New Mobe), founded in October of 1969 around a commitment to hold a massive but peaceful demonstration the following month. Dellinger led the New Mobe along with several moderates. They coordinated planning for the demonstration with the Vietnam Moratorium Committee (VMC), an organization founded by people in the orbit of Al Lowenstein and Eugene McCarthy, as well as Stewart Meacham, a Quaker who had conceived the dramatic March Against Death. The liberals in the VMC were suspicious of allying with radical pacifists, but the attempt at rapprochement with liberal doves signified a genuine return to the center for many in the Mobe.

The timing for such an action was perfect. During the summer, SDS had held its last national convention, which was so chaotic and extreme that the organization simply splintered out of existence. Although events would galvanize renewed unrest on campuses in 1970, the national organizations of the student Left were largely defunct and discredited after 1969, leaving liberals as the only plausible coalition partners for the Mobe's antiwar leaders. Then in early November President Nixon delivered a national address in which he asserted that a "silent majority" of Americans supported his policies in Vietnam. This speech was delivered at a time when polls showed a developing majority of Americans opposed to the war. Nixon's speech drew lines that forced liberals and radical pacifist antiwar leaders more clearly, albeit shakily, into the same camp and set their determination to harness and demonstrate the opposition to the war felt in culturally mainstream sectors of American society.

On that Saturday, November 15, several hundred thousand participants listened to a plethora of speakers that included Dave Dellinger and Senators Eugene McCarthy and George McGovern, a platform organized by Brad Lyttle. The predominantly peaceful and festive spirit of the day was accentuated by its music, which included performances by Pete Seeger, the group Peter, Paul, and Mary, and Arlo Guthrie.

The November Mobilization, then, betokened a new desire on the part of many—though not all—radical pacifists to forge antiwar coalitions with liberal doves and to return to such traditional peace movement methods as marches and vigils. In a sense, these radical pacifists had come full circle by 1970. No longer envisioning revolution after the events of the late 1960s, increasing numbers of peace activists settled into organizing protests with the feel of a large outing for diverse groups of people whose politics were often no more revolutionary than a shared opposition to the government's policies in Vietnam.

Radical pacifism's impact upon protest movements in the era after World War II has left an ambivalent legacy. Radical pacifist groups played an instrumental role in defining the methods, organizational structure, and ethos of postwar dissent. During this period, they established nonviolent direct action as a major protest method on the American Left, and many of their leaders became key figures in the reconstitution of American dissent during the 1950s and 1960s. Yet, in the end, the movements radical pacifists led or influenced proved far more adept at challenging and disrupting the institutions or policies they deemed unjust than in creating sustainable alternatives. And the decentralism and nonexclusion that radical pacifists embraced rendered their organizational vehicles vulnerable to the destructive sectarianism that reemerged on the Left in the late 1960s.

The radical pacifist program of direct action, decentralism, and participatory democracy within organizations has continued to deeply inform American protest since the Vietnam era, as is evident in the history of the antinuclear and environmental movements of recent decades. Nonviolent direct action is often used today by groups on both the Left and the Right whose leaders have little or no knowledge of radical pacifist history. The forms, if not always the spirit, of radical pacifism have become paradigmatic for grassroots dissent in contemporary American society. Perhaps this is because the radical pacifist style allows activists to remain immersed within a libertarian tradition around which there is much consensual agreement while challenging public opinion on particular social issues. Yet the American Left today is also disjointed, episodic, and obsessed with individualistic lifestyle concerns. Perhaps this, too, is at least in part a legacy of radical pacifist history.

Notes

ONE

1. See David Dellinger, *From Yale to Jail: The Life Story of a Moral Dissenter* (New York: Pantheon Books, 1993), p. 63.

2. The Union Eight were Donald Benedict, Joseph J. Bevilacqua, Meredith Dallas, Dave Dellinger, George Houser, William H. Lovell, Howard E. Spragg, and Richard J. Wichlei.

3. Reinhold Niebuhr to DeWitte Wyckoff, November 18, 1940, Swarthmore College Peace Collection (SCPC), Fellowship of Reconciliation (FOR) MSS, Box 18.

4. Reinhold Niebuhr to A. J. Muste, December 26, 1940, SCPC, FOR MSS, Box 18.

5. "A Christian Conviction on Conscription and Registration," public statement of eight students at Union Theological Seminary, October 10, 1940, published by the Fellowship of Reconciliation and other peace organizations, SCPC, FOR MSS, Box 18. Selected text of the statement also appears in Staughton Lynd, ed., *Nonviolence in America: A Documentary History* (New York: Bobbs-Merrill, 1966), pp. 296–99.

6. Roy Finch, "Comments on WRL Policy and Program," SCPC, War Resisters League (WRL) MSS, Series A, Box 2.

7. David Dellinger, *From Yale to Jail,* p. 85.

8. On Gandhi, see Mohandas K. Gandhi, *An Autobiography, or The Story of My Experiments with Truth* (Ahmedabad: Navajivan Publishing House, 1956); Louis Fischer, *The Life of Mahatma Gandhi* (New York: Harper and Bros., 1950); and Erik Erikson, *Gandhi's Truth: On the Origins of Militant Nonviolence* (New York: W. W. Norton, 1969).

9. See author's interview with Marjorie Swann, 4/1/91. Also see Marjorie Swann, "Following the Vision: Fifty Years in the Nonviolent Movement," *On the Issues* 11 (1989): 22–30. See also Joann Ooiman Robinson, *Abraham Went Out: A Biography of A. J. Muste* (Philadelphia: Temple University Press, 1981), p. 16; Taylor Branch, *Parting the Waters: America in the King Years, 1954–1963* (New York: Simon and Schuster, 1988), pp. 73–75, 262–63; and Aldon D. Morris, *The Origins of the Civil Rights Movement: Black Communities Organizing for Change* (New York: Free Press, 1984), p. 97, for the continuing influence of Social Gospel theology on twentieth-century liberal Protestantism, especially with regard to race relations.

10. On the Old Left's organizing efforts around race, see Robin D. G. Kelley, *Hammer and Hoe: Alabama Communists during the Great Depression* (Chapel Hill, NC: University of North Carolina Press, 1990); Robert Korstad and Nelson Lichtenstein, "Opportunities Found and Lost: Labor, Radicals, and the Early Civil Rights Movement," *Journal of American History* 75 (December 1988): 786–811; and Gerald Horne, *Communist Front: The Civil Rights Congress, 1946–1956* (East Rutherford, NJ: Fairleigh Dickinson University Press, 1988).

11. Author's interview with Bill Sutherland, 11/4/90.

12. See Lawrence S. Wittner, *Rebels against War: The American Peace Movement, 1933–1983* (Philadelphia: Temple University Press, 1984), pp. 6–7; Ralph S. Brax, *The First Student Movement: Student Activism in the United States during the 1930s* (Port Washington, NY: Kennikat Press, 1981), pp. 36–37; and Robert Cohen, *When the Old Left Was Young: Student Radicals and America's First Mass Student Movement, 1929–1941* (New York: Oxford University Press, 1993).

13. Howard M. Bell, *Youth Tell Their Story: A Study of the Conditions and Attitudes of Young People in Maryland between the Ages of 16 and 24* (Washington, D.C.: American Council on Education, 1938), pp. 240–46.

14. *New York Times,* October 31, 1940.

15. Jacquelyn S. Nelson argues in *Indiana Quakers Confront the Civil War* (Indianapolis: Indiana Historical Society, 1991) that many young Quaker men nonetheless chose to participate in the Civil War on the Union side.

16. On the treatment of C.O.s during World War I, see Albert N. Keim and Grant M. Stoltzfus, *The Politics of Conscience: The Historic Peace Churches and America at War, 1917–1955* (Scottsdale, PA: Herald Press, 1988); and Charles DeBenedetti, *The Peace Reform in American History* (Bloomington: Indiana University Press, 1980).

17. See Dellinger, *From Yale to Jail*, p. 78.

18. "A Christian Conviction on Conscription and Registration," public

statement of eight students at Union Theological Seminary, October 10, 1940, SCPC, FOR MSS, Box 18.

19. See Dellinger, *From Yale to Jail*, p. 420; author's interview with George Houser, 10/4/94.

20. See author's interview with Dave Dellinger, 6/16/93; and author's interview with George Houser, 10/4/94.

TWO

1. See Mulford Sibley and Asa Wardlaw, "Conscientious Objectors in Prison," in Staughton Lynd, ed., *Nonviolence in America: A Documentary History* (New York: Bobbs-Merrill, 1966).

2. Harold Schoenfeld, "The Danbury Story," in Peter Mayer, ed., *The Pacifist Conscience* (New York: Holt, Rinehart, and Winston, 1966), pp. 332–34.

3. National Service Board for Religious Objectors, *Directory of Civilian Public Service: May, 1941 to March, 1947* (Washington, D.C.: NSBRO, 1947), pp. x–xix. These C.O.s were those who did not serve in the military in any capacity, not to be confused with the approximately 25,000 who were classified 1-A-O, willing to take noncombatant military assignments.

4. Ibid., pp. xviii–xix.

5. The study published in 1948 by Ray R. Kelley and Paul E. Johnson, both of the Department of Psychology at Boston University, "Emotional Traits in Pacifists," *Journal of Social Psychology* 28 (1948): 275–86, is hampered by its bias throughout that pacifism is psychological deviance, and by the fact that the authors only studied six men in any detail and built most of their article on the psychological analysis of one man. In addition, their conclusion is so vague as to be meaningless (see p. 285). The National Service Board for Religious Objectors did not do its own systematic study until the 1990 pamphlet, *Civilian Public Servants: A Report on 210 World War II Conscientious Objectors*, by Paul A. Wilhelm (Washington, D.C.: National Interreligious Service Board for Conscientious Objectors [the direct descendant of NSBRO]). This study was based upon the reflections of 210 men over four decades after being in CPS and is more anecdotal than systematic.

6. Adrian E. Gory and David C. McClelland, "Characteristics of Conscientious Objectors in World War II," *Journal of Consulting Psychology* 11, no. 5 (September–October 1947): 245–57. This article, too, is biased insofar as Gory had worked in the personnel department of CPS and McClelland had worked for the American Friends Service Committee during the war. Despite the fact that both were professors at Wesleyan University at the time of publication and had not submitted their article to the AFSC for its imprimatur, the article exhibits a strong empathy with the pacifist position. Nonetheless, the data appears to have been rigorously compiled. In addition, its focus on Friends camps, where the most political activity in CPS occurred during the war, is

useful for the present study. Also useful is Gordon Zahn, "A Descriptive Study of the Social Backgrounds of Conscientious Objectors during World War II" (Ph.D. dissertation, Catholic University of America, 1953). Zahn had been director of a CPS camp in Maryland.

7. "Pangs of Conscience," *Washington Post,* November 22, 1944.

8. Lillian Schlissel, *Conscience in America: A Documentary History of Conscientious Objection in America, 1757–1967* (New York: E. P. Dutton and Co., 1968), p. 215.

9. See Wittner, *Rebels against War,* p. 84.

10. Information taken from A. J. Muste letter to "Friend" (salutation used by Muste in general letters to Fellowship of Reconciliation members) June 12, 1942, SCPC, FOR MSS, Box 17.

11. Dellinger letter quoted in Muste letter to "Friend," June 12, 1942.

12. Quoted in letter from A. J. Muste to Francis Biddle, June 17, 1942, SCPC, FOR MSS, Box 17.

13. Author's interview with Bill Sutherland, 11/4/90.

14. Author's interview with Bull Sutherland, 11/4/90. See also Dellinger, *From Yale to Jail,* pp. 119–20.

15. Dave Dellinger, reply to letter in *Alternative* I, no. 4 (July–August 1948): 5. See also Dellinger, *From Yale to Jail,* pp. 121–22.

16. Author's interview with Bill Sutherland, 11/4/90.

17. *The Absolutist,* no. 10, November 16, 1943, Hoover Institution Archives, FOR (USA) MSS, Box 19.

18. George Houser to A. J. Muste, June 11, 1941, SCPC, FOR MSS, Box 17.

19. George Houser, *CORE: A Brief History,* pamphlet published by CORE in 1949, p. 1, SCPC, CORE MSS.

20. August Meier and Elliot Rudwick, *CORE: A Study in the Civil Rights Movement* (New York: Oxford University Press, 1973), p. 5.

21. CORE has been justly praised for its germinal role in the tactical development of the black freedom struggles of the 1950s and 1960s. What has often not been recognized is the fact that it arose in large part, and was maintained for over fifteen years, due to the efforts of radical pacifists closely linked with the FOR. See also James Farmer, *Lay Bare the Heart: An Autobiography of the Civil Rights Movement* (New York: Arbor House, 1985).

22. James Farmer, "Memorandum to A. J. Muste on Provisional Plans for Brotherhood Mobilization," January 8, 1942, SCPC, FOR MSS, Box 7. See also Peter Mayer, ed., *The Pacifist Conscience* (New York: Holt, Rinehart, and Winston, 1966), pp. 363–65. Mayer dates the memorandum February 19, 1942, but January 8 is probably the correct date, for Muste responded by letter January 19.

23. On Muste, see Joann Ooiman Robinson, *Abraham Went Out: A Biography of A. J. Muste* (Philadelphia: Temple University Press, 1981); Nat Hentoff, *Peace Agitator: The Story of A. J. Muste* (New York: Macmillan, 1963).

24. Robinson, *Abraham Went Out*, p. 80.

25. *Time*, July 10, 1939, p. 37.

26. On Randolph, see Paula F. Pfeffer, *A. Philip Randolph, Pioneer of the Civil Rights Movement* (Baton Rouge: Louisiana State University Press, 1990); Jervis Anderson, *A. Philip Randolph: A Biographical Portrait* (New York: Harcourt Brace Jovanovich, 1973).

27. James Farmer, *Lay Bare the Heart: An Autobiography of the Civil Rights Movement* (New York: Arbor House, 1985), p. 89.

28. A. J. Muste to John Swomley, February 1, 1945, SCPC, FOR MSS, Box 7, Farmer correspondence folder.

29. A. J. Muste to James Farmer, January 19, 1942, SCPC, FOR MSS, Box 7, Farmer correspondence folder.

30. See Farmer, *Lay Bare the Heart*, pp. 85–86.

31. See A. J. Muste to George Houser, June 25, 1941 (when Houser was still in Danbury), SCPC, FOR MSS, Box 17.

32. "An Open Letter to the FOR," signed by Dave Dellinger, Bill Sutherland, and fourteen other imprisoned C.O.s, February 3, 1944. An exchange of letters followed: Muste to Dellinger, April 4, 1944; "An Open Letter to the FOR," signed by Dave Dellinger and eleven other imprisoned C.O.s, announcing their resignation from the FOR, because they felt it was "a sweet-smelling flower in the lapel of the privileged classes," June 3, 1944; A. J. Muste to Dave Dellinger "and Friends," July 5, 1944. SCPC, FOR MSS, Box 19, Lewisburg folder.

33. George Houser, *CORE: A Brief History*, p. 3.

34. Information for descriptions of this and other CORE actions is drawn largely from *Cracking the Color Line*, a history published by CORE in 1960, SCPC, CORE MSS; George Houser, *Erasing the Color Line* (New York: Fellowship Publications, 1945); George Houser, *CORE: A Brief History*, pamphlet published by CORE in 1949, SCPC, CORE MSS; and August Meier and Elliot Rudwick, *CORE: A Study in the Civil Rights Movement*.

35. Author's interview with Bill Sutherland, 11/12/90.

36. Author's interview with Dave McReynolds, 10/16/94.

37. Author's interview with Bill Sutherland, 11/12/90.

38. Bayard Rustin, "Non-Violence vs. Jim Crow," *Fellowship* (July 1942).

39. John Nevin Sayre to Julia Davis Rustin (Bayard Rustin's grandmother), March 9, 1944, SCPC, FOR MSS, unprocessed file.

40. See Minutes of the "First National Planning Conference of the Committee of Racial Equality," June 10, 1943, SCPC, CORE MSS.

41. Jay Holmes Smith to A. J. Muste, July 8, 1943, SCPC, FOR MSS, March on Washington folder.

42. A. J. Muste to A. Philip Randolph, January 11, 1943, SCPC, FOR MSS, March on Washington folder.

43. See Wittner, *Rebels against War*, pp. 65–66; Robinson, *Abraham Went Out*, p. 112.

44. "Civil Disobedience: Is It the Answer to Jim Crow?" undated (probably 1943), published by Non-Violent Direct Action News, SCPC, Muste MSS, microfilm reel 89.4.

45. See John Hope Franklin and Alfred A. Moss, Jr., *From Slavery to Freedom: A History of Negro Americans* (New York: Alfred A. Knopf, 1988), p. 399; and Pfeffer, *A. Philip Randolph,* p. 48.

46. Farmer, "Memorandum," January 8, 1942.

47. George Houser, "Memo on a Mass Non-Violent Interracial Movement," undated (probably 1943), SCPC, CORE MSS.

48. Penina M. Glazer, "A Decade of Transition: A Study of Radical Journals of the 1940s," (Ph.D. dissertation, Rutgers University, 1970), p. ii.

49. Jim Peck, *We Who Would Not Kill* (New York: Lyle Stuart, 1958), p. 121.

50. Ibid., pp. 68–69.

51. See author's interview with Bill Sutherland, 11/12/90.

52. Peck, *We Who Would Not Kill,* p. 174.

53. Bennett and superintendent quoted in Wittner, *Rebels against War,* p. 91.

54. *The Absolutist,* no. 10, November 16, 1943, Hoover Institution Archives, FOR (USA) MSS, Box 19.

55. See, for instance, Alan Trachtenberg, *The Incorporation of America: Culture and Society in the Gilded Age* (New York: Hill and Wang, 1982); and Robert H. Wiebe, *The Search for Order, 1877–1920* (New York: Hill and Wang, 1967).

56. "Decentralized Democratic Socialism," memo of Committee for Nonviolent Revolution, probably 1946, Resource Center for Nonviolence, Kepler MSS, Box 1.

57. "Letter from Lewis Hill, Received too Late to Be Incorporated in Preconference Report," August 4, 1947, SCPC, Committee for Nonviolent Revolution folder.

58. Comment by Dave Dellinger in "A Discussion of Problems in Nonviolent Revolution," 1945, SCPC, Committee for Nonviolent Revolution folder.

59. Dwight Macdonald, "By Way of Rejoinder," *Politics* 1, no. 6 (July 1944): 179–80. On Macdonald's identification with radical pacifists, see also Michael Wreszin, *A Rebel in Defense of Tradition: The Life and Politics of Dwight Macdonald* (New York: Basic Books, 1994), 191–93.

60. *Directory of Civilian Public Service,* p. xviii.

61. Purnell Benson to A. J. Muste, "Corbett Bishop Summary," July 19, 1945, SCPC, FOR MSS, Box 14.

62. Ibid.

63. Information taken from Wittner, *Rebels against War,* pp. 89–90.

64. Quoted in James P. Mullin, Secretary of Prison Service Committee, "Report of Secretary's Visit with Corbett Bishop in Philadelphia County Jail, March 15, 1945," April 1945, SCPC, FOR MSS, Box 14.

65. Details of Bishop's arrival at Macedonia taken from Art Wiser letter to author, May 1995. Wiser joined the Macedonia Community shortly after Bishop's arrival.

66. See Wittner, *Rebels against War,* pp. 78–79.

67. See, for instance, Herbert G. Gutman, *The Black Family in Slavery and Freedom, 1750–1925* (New York: Pantheon Books, 1976); Eugene D. Genovese, *Roll, Jordan, Roll: The World the Slaves Made* (New York: Vintage Books, 1974); and Kenneth M. Stampp, *The Peculiar Institution: Slavery in the Ante-Bellum South* (New York: Knopf, 1956).

68. See, for instance, *Germfask Newsletter* 2, no. 5 (October 1945), Resource Center for Nonviolence, Kepler MSS, Box 3.

69. Ibid., vol. 3, no. 1 (January 1946).

70. See, for instance, ibid., vol. 3, no. 5 (May 1946).

71. "Reports of Superintendents of State Mental Hospitals on the Work of Conscientious Objectors, 1943–45," in Lillian Schlissel, ed., *Conscience in America,* p. 236.

72. *Germfask Newsletter* 3, no. 5 (May 1946).

73. "C.O.s in the News: Good or Bad?" undated Big Flats newsletter, Resource Center for Nonviolence, Kepler MSS, Box 1.

74. Roy Finch, Lew Hill, et al., to David Dellinger, et al., April 27, 1945, SCPC, FOR MSS, Box 6.

THREE

1. Richard H. Pells, *The Liberal Mind in a Conservative Age: American Intellectuals in the 1940s and 1950s* (Middletown, CT: Wesleyan University Press, 1989), p. 45.

2. Dwight Macdonald, front-page editorial, *Politics* 2, no. 8 (August 1945).

3. David Dellinger, "Declaration of War," *Direct Action* 1, no. 1 (Autumn 1945): 6–9.

4. Quoted in John Whiting, "The Lengthening Shadow: Lewis Hill and the Origins of Listener-Sponsored Broadcasting in America," in "Cracking the Ike Age: Aspects of Fifties America," *The Dolphin,* no. 23 (Autumn 1992) (Aarhus, Denmark: Aarhus University Press), p. 183. See also material on Lewis Hill at Pacifica National Office, Berkeley, CA.

5. "The February Conference on Non-Violent Revolutionary Socialism: A Discussion of Problems in Non-Violent Revolution," SCPC, Committee for Non-Violent Revolution (CNVR) folder.

6. See "Report on Decentralized Democratic Socialism: Final Statement Adopted by Conference," in "Reports of the February Conference on Non-Violent Revolution Held at Chicago, January 6–9, 1946," SCPC, CNVR folder.

7. See George E. Hopkins, "Bombing and the American Conscience during World War II," *The Historian* 28, no. 3 (May 1966): 451–73. See also Bar-

ton J. Bernstein, "The Atomic Bombings Reconsidered," *Foreign Affairs* 74, no. 1 (January/February 1995): 146.

8. Hadley Cantril, ed., *Public Opinion, 1935–1946* (Princeton, NJ: Princeton University Press, 1951), pp. 20–23.

9. Neil H. Katz, "Radical Pacifism and the Contemporary American Peace Movement: The Committee for Nonviolent Action, 1957–1967" (Ph.D. dissertation, University of Maryland, 1974), pp. 7–8.

10. Lew Hill to Roy Kepler, March 6, 1948, Kepler MSS, Resource Center for Nonviolence, Santa Cruz, CA, Box 1.

11. "Where Radicalism in the Next Five Years," minutes of a CNVR conference held August 8–10, 1947, SCPC, CNVR folder.

12. *Bulletin* of CNVR, vol. 2, no. 1, September 1, 1947.

13. Ammon Hennacy, "Ammon Hennacy to the Tax Gatherer," *The Peace-maker* 1, no. 10, January 30, 1950: 4.

14. George Houser, "A Personal Retrospective on the 1947 Journey of Reconciliation," in George Houser's personal files, used with author's permission.

15. A. J. Muste to George Houser, January 11, 1944, SCPC, FOR MSS, Box 8.

16. Quoted from "Interracial Workshop Progress Report," probably printed by the FOR and CORE in 1947, SCPC, CORE MSS.

17. See author's interview with George Houser, 10/4/94.

18. Houser, "Personal Retrospective."

19. Information taken from George Houser and Bayard Rustin, *We Challenged Jim Crow!: A Report on the Journey of Reconciliation, April 9–23, 1947,* published jointly by the FOR and CORE in 1947, SCPC, CORE MSS.

20. See, for instance, CNVR mailing to Ellen Starr Brinton, December 17, 1947, SCPC, CNVR folder.

21. Resolution quoted in Wittner, *Rebels against War,* p. 153.

22. Abe Kaufman to Sidney Aberman, February 12, 1951, SCPC, WRL MSS, Series B, Box 10.

23. Ibid., November 10, 1950, SCPC, WRL MSS, Series A, Box 2.

24. Roy Kepler, "WRL Program and Relationship to FOR," undated, SCPC, WRL MSS, Series A, Box 2.

25. Roy Kepler, "Memorandum on WRL Policy and Program," undated, SCPC, WRL MSS, Series A, Box 2.

26. Roy Kepler to "Johnny," (form letter to friends, with salutation penciled in), February 29, 1948, Kepler MSS, Resource Center for Nonviolence, Box 1.

27. Lew Hill to Roy Kepler, March 6, 1948, Kepler MSS, Resource Center for Nonviolence, Box 1.

28. On Kepler, see author's interview with Ira Sandperl, 3/13/91.

29. See KPFA Program Folio, February 17–March 2, 1957, Pacifica National Office, Berkeley, CA.

30. "Call for a Conference on More Disciplined and Revolutionary Pacifist Activity," 1948, Kepler MSS, Resource Center for Nonviolence, Box 1.

31. "Report on Basis of Membership Adopted at Peacemakers National Conference," April 1–3, 1949, Kepler MSS, Resource Center for Nonviolence, Box 1.

32. "Peacemakers: What Is It?" undated pamphlet, SCPC, WRL MSS, Series B, Box 10.

33. A. J. Muste, "Build the Non-Violent Revolutionary Movement—Now," undated, Kepler MSS, Peacemakers Folder, Resource Center for Nonviolence, Box 1.

34. "Proceedings of National Committee of Peacemakers," December 28–30, 1948, Kepler MSS, Resource Center for Nonviolence, Box 1.

35. "A World Non-Violent Revolutionary Movement," May 1951, Kepler MSS, Resource Center for Nonviolence, Box 1.

36. Membership data taken from Peacemakers Executive Committee Minutes, October 10, 1949, Kepler MSS, Resource Center for Nonviolence, Box 1.

37. "Call to a Conference on Non-Violent Civil Disobedience to the Draft," 1948, Kepler MSS, Resource Center for Nonviolence, Box 1.

38. See Wittner, *Rebels against War,* p. 163; and Wreszin, *A Rebel in Defense of Tradition,* p. 192.

39. For more on the league, see Pfeffer, *A. Philip Randolph;* and Robinson, *Abraham Went Out.*

40. See "Peacemakers Executive Committee Meeting," January 11, 1949, Kepler MSS, Resource Center for Nonviolence, Box 1.

41. See Peacemakers Executive Committee Minutes for January 24, 1949, and January 31, 1949, as well as the Peacemakers *Bulletin,* December 10, 1948, Kepler MSS, Resource Center for Nonviolence, Box 1.

42. See "Dear Fellowship Member," letter from A. J. Muste to FOR members, June 3, 1949, Kepler MSS, Resource Center for Nonviolence, Box 1; Minutes of Peacemakers National Executive Committee Meeting, June 6, 1949, Kepler MSS, Resource Center for Nonviolence, Box 1; and letter from Joint Committee for Gara Demonstration (headed by Roy Kepler) to President Truman, July 25, 1949, SCPC, Peacemakers box.

43. See *Cleveland Plain Dealer,* March 12, 1951; and "Pacifist Sends Copy of Gospels and Thoreau's Essay on Civil Disobedience to Collector of Internal Revenue," March 12, 1951, SCPC, Peacemakers box.

44. On Dorothy Day, Ammon Hennacy, and the Catholic Worker, see Robert Coles, *Dorothy Day: A Radical Devotion* (Reading, MA: Addison-Wesley, 1987); James Forest, *Love Is the Measure: A Biography of Dorothy Day* (New York: Paulist Press, 1986); Anne Klejment, *Dorothy Day and the Catholic Worker: A Bibliography* (New York: Garland, 1986); and Rosalie Riegle Troester, ed., *Voices from the Catholic Worker* (Philadelphia: Temple University Press, 1993).

45. See "Handbook on Nonpayment of Taxes," undated Peacemakers

publication (probably 1965), Kepler MSS, Resource Center for Nonviolence, Box 1, Peacemakers folder.

46. See Jim Peck, *The Proof of the Pudding,* 1949 CORE pamphlet, reprinted from *The Crisis* (November 1949), SCPC, CORE MSS. On CORE actions in the late 1940s, see also Jim Peck, *Bilboism in New Jersey,* undated CORE pamphlet, reprinted from *The Crisis* (January 1948), SCPC, CORE MSS; George Houser, *Project: Brotherhood,* 1952 CORE pamphlet, reprinted from *Fellowship,* SCPC, CORE MSS; and *Cracking the Color Line,* 1960 CORE pamphlet written by Jim Peck, SCPC, CORE MSS.

47. See Meier and Rudwick, *CORE,* pp. 54–57.

48. A. J. Muste, "Peace Fronts Today," May 1951, SCPC, FOR MSS, Box 4.

49. "Statement on Civil Rights," October 30, 1949, SCPC, WRL MSS, Series A, Box 2.

50. Minutes of the FOR Executive Committee Meeting, February 1, 1954, SCPC, FOR MSS, Box 4.

51. Author's interview with Bill Sutherland, 11/4/90.

52. On the European bicycle trip, see Dellinger, *From Yale to Jail,* pp. 158–70; also author's interview with Dave Dellinger, 6/16/93, author's interview with Bill Sutherland, 11/4/90, and author's interview with Ralph DiGia, 3/23/91.

53. Copy of leaflet later distributed by Peacemakers as a pamphlet, undated, SCPC, WRL MSS, Series B, Box 10. See also A. J. Muste, "Peacemakers Message Still Getting under Iron Curtain," February 11, 1952, SCPC, WRL MSS, Series B, Box 10; and Dellinger, *From Yale to Jail,* pp. 472–73.

54. Sutherland quoted in Dellinger, *From Yale to Jail,* p. 168.

55. Author's interview with Bill Sutherland, 11/4/90.

56. Sutherland quoted in Dellinger, *From Yale to Jail,* p. 169. See also author's interview with Dave Dellinger, 5/17/95.

57. Minutes of Peacemakers Executive Committee Meetings, February 22, 1952, and February 28, 1952, SCPC, WRL MSS, Series B, Box 10.

58. Author's interviews with Bill Sutherland, 11/4/90 and 11/12/90.

59. Author's interview with George Houser, 10/4/94.

60. See George Houser, *No One Can Stop the Rain: Glimpses of Africa's Liberation Struggle* (New York: Pilgrim Press, 1989).

61. Fisher remained in the labor movement until her death at the age of forty-nine (author's interview with George Houser, 10/4/94).

62. See Meier and Rudwick, *CORE,* p. 73.

FOUR

1. "Peacemaker Statement on Community," June 1952, SCPC, Peacemakers Box.

2. See Roy McCorkel, "Vocations for Pacifists," undated, Kepler MSS, Resource Center for Nonviolence, Box 1, Peacemakers folder.

3. See Dellinger, *From Yale to Jail,* p. 150.

4. See ibid., p. 170.

5. Ibid., p. 173.

6. Ibid., p. 172.

7. Untitled CNVR pamphlet, SCPC, CNVR folder.

8. "An Open Letter to Young Men," undated Peacemakers pamphlet, Kepler MSS, Resource Center for Nonviolence, Box 1.

9. "A Message to Those of Our Fellow Americans Who Practice or Profess Religion," undated Peacemakers open letter, Kepler MSS, Resource Center for Nonviolence, Box 1. Emphasis added.

10. Radical pacifists also shared this contradiction with much of the leadership of the Left in the 1960s. See Sara Evans, *Personal Politics: The Roots of Women's Liberation in the Civil Rights Movement and the New Left* (New York: Random House, 1980).

11. Author's interview with Ralph DiGia, 3/23/91.

12. Swann quoted in Bruce Tober, "Marjorie Swann: Pacifist," *The World: Journal of the Unitarian Universalist Association* 5, no. 1 (January/February 1991), p. 16.

13. Much of Swann's biographical information taken from author's interview with Marjorie Swann, 4/1/91.

14. "Dear Peacemakers and Friends," letter from Marjorie Swann, August 15, 1953, SCPC, WRL MSS, Series B, Box 10.

15. A court later ordered Lynd's discharge changed to honorable.

16. The Lynds were best known for their influential book, *Middletown: A Study in Modern American Culture* (New York: Harcourt, Brace, and World, 1929).

17. Author's interview with Tom Cornell, 5/6/95.

18. See author's interview with Staughton Lynd, 3/9/91.

19. Dave Dellinger, "The Community Was Made for Man," pp. 18–19, and Staughton Lynd, "The Individual Was Made for Community," in *Liberation* (January 1957): 15–18.

20. Author's interview with Dave McReynolds, 10/16/94.

21. See author's interview with Ralph DiGia, 3/23/91.

22. Author's interview with Bill Sutherland, 11/12/90.

23. Untitled FOR statement adopted by the FOR Executive Committee, 1/28/53. SCPC, FOR MSS.

24. Author's interview with Ralph DiGia, 3/23/91.

25. See Todd Gitlin, *The Sixties: Years of Hope, Days of Rage* (New York: Bantam Books, 1989), pp. 31–54.

26. A. J. Muste, *Gandhi and the H-Bomb: How Nonviolence Can Take the Place of War* (Nyack, NY: Fellowship Publications, [1950] 1983), p. 3.

27. A. J. Muste, "Proposal for a Bi-Monthly Magazine," February 21,

1955, SCPC, WRL MSS, Series B, Box 12. See also "Monthly Magazine Prospectus," 1955, SCPC, WRL MSS, Series B, Box 12.

28. Dellinger, *From Yale to Jail*, p. 149.

29. Author's interview with Dave McReynolds, 10/16/94.

30. Muste was also on the editorial board of *Dissent*.

31. A. J. Muste, "Proposal for a Bi-Monthly Magazine," February 21, 1955, SCPC, WRL MSS, Series B, Box 12.

32. "Tract for the Times," *Liberation* 1, no. 1 (March 1956): 3.

33. Irwin Unger, *The Movement: A History of the American New Left, 1959–1972* (New York: Harper and Row, 1974), p. 17.

34. Wittner, *Rebels against War*, p. 237.

35. Dave McReynolds recalls warmly: "That's an education in itself. . . . To sit every Wednesday in a discussion with Muste, Finch, Rustin, and Dellinger." Author's interview with Dave McReynolds, 10/16/94.

36. See Aldon D. Morris, *The Origins of the Civil Rights Movement: Black Communities Organizing for Change* (New York: Free Press, 1984).

37. "Proposal for Christian Pacifist Work in the South," 1954, SCPC, FOR MSS, unprocessed race material.

38. On Smiley, see David L. Chappell, *Inside Agitators: White Southerners in the Civil Rights Movement* (Baltimore: Johns Hopkins University Press, 1994), pp. 58–61.

39. See Al Hassler to Glenn Smiley, November 5, 1955, SCPC, FOR MSS, unprocessed race material.

40. Letter from Glenn Smiley, December 5, 1955, SCPC, FOR MSS, unprocessed race material.

41. See letter from Matthew D. McCollom, 1958, SCPC, FOR MSS, unprocessed race material.

42. On the Montgomery Bus Boycott, see Martin Luther King, Jr., *Stride toward Freedom: The Montgomery Story* (New York: Harper and Brothers, 1958); David J. Garrow, *Bearing the Cross: Martin Luther King, Jr., and the Southern Christian Leadership Conference* (New York: Random House, 1988); Taylor Branch, *Parting the Waters: America in the King Years, 1954–63* (New York: Simon and Schuster, 1988); and David J. Garrow, ed., *The Walking City: The Montgomery Bus Boycott, 1955–1956*, vol. 7 in the series entitled *Martin Luther King, Jr., and the Civil Rights Movement* (New York: Carlson Publishing, 1989).

43. See, for instance, John Swomley to Wilson Riles, 2/21/56, SCPC, FOR MSS, unprocessed race material.

44. Glenn Smiley to John Swomley and Al Hassler, February 29, 1956, SCPC, FOR MSS, unprocessed race material.

45. See Garrow, *Bearing the Cross*, p. 68.

46. Smiley to Swomley and Hassler, 2/29/56.

47. See Charles Walker to Bayard Rustin, 11/14/49, SCPC, FOR MSS, Box 4; see also Martin Luther King, Jr., *Stride toward Freedom*, p. 95. Walker's

letter, written shortly after Muste's talk at Crozer, does not support the recollection of that evening by one of Garrow's sources. It would appear King and Muste did not argue at the talk. See Garrow, *Bearing the Cross,* p. 41.

48. King, *Stride toward Freedom,* p. 96.

49. On the development of King's religious thinking, see John J. Ansbro, *Martin Luther King, Jr.: The Making of a Mind* (Maryknoll, NY: Orbis Books, 1982); James Cone, *Martin and Malcolm and America: A Dream or a Nightmare* (Maryknoll, NY: Orbis Books, 1991); and Kenneth L. Smith and Ira G. Zepp, *Search for the Beloved Community: The Thinking of Martin Luther King, Jr.* (Valley Forge, PA: Judson Press, 1980).

50. See King speech quoted in *The Montgomery Advertiser,* January 31, 1956.

51. Smith and Zepp, *Search for the Beloved Community,* p. 71.

52. King, *Stride toward Freedom,* p. 99.

53. See Garrow, *Bearing the Cross,* p. 62.

54. See ibid., pp. 72–73.

55. Smiley to Swomley and Hassler, 2/29/56.

56. See, for instance, John Swomley to Glenn Smiley, 2/29/56, SCPC, FOR MSS, unprocessed race.

57. Smiley letter quoted in Garrow, *Bearing the Cross,* p. 70.

58. See ibid., p. 73.

59. King, *Stride toward Freedom,* p. 101.

60. Ibid.

61. Bayard Rustin, "Report on Montgomery, Alabama," March 21, 1956, published by War Resisters League, SCPC, FOR MSS, unprocessed race material.

62. "Saddle Bags," FOR memo from Glenn Smiley, March 4, 1956, SCPC, FOR MSS, unprocessed race material.

63. Muste quoted in "Report from the South, Number 2," Glenn Smiley, August 15, 1956, SCPC, FOR MSS, unprocessed race material.

64. "Report from the South, Number 2," Glenn Smiley, August 15, 1956, SCPC, FOR MSS, unprocessed race material.

65. See King, *Stride toward Freedom,* p. 101.

66. See author's interview with Ira Sandperl, 3/13/91.

67. "Report from the South, Number 2," Glenn Smiley, August 15, 1956, SCPC, FOR MSS, unprocessed race material.

68. Glenn Smiley to Vera Britain, December 4, 1963, SCPC, FOR MSS, unprocessed race material.

69. See Smiley's reflections on this in "Proposal on Race Relations Activities in the Fellowship of Reconciliation to Be Presented to Foundations for Possible Support," Glenn Smiley, 1966, SCPC, FOR MSS, unprocessed race material.

70. Bayard Rustin, "From Protest to Politics: The Future of the Civil Rights Movement," *Commentary* 39, no. 2 (February 1965): 25–31.

71. On the beginnings of the SCLC, see Adam Fairclough, *To Redeem the*

Soul of America: The Southern Christian Leadership Conference and Martin Luther King, Jr. (Athens: University of Georgia Press, 1987).

FIVE

1. Unattributed first-hand account, probably Lawrence Scott, "The Nevada Witness," SCPC, Scott MSS, Box 2, Nevada folder.

2. James Peck, "Trespassing on the Bomb Site," *Liberation* 2, no. 6 (September 1957): 8–9.

3. On Bigelow's conversion to pacifism, see Albert S. Bigelow, "Why I Am Sailing into the Pacific Bomb-Test Area," *Liberation* 2, no. 11 (February 1958): 4–8.

4. Lawrence Scott, "Words Are Not Enough," *Liberation* 2, no. 3 (May 1957): 14–15.

5. For convenience, the organization will be referred to as CNVA in the text even during the period when it was still NVAANW.

6. On CNVA and SANE, see Wittner, *Rebels against War,* pp. 242 ff.; Maurice Isserman, *If I Had a Hammer: The Death of the Old Left and the Birth of the New Left* (New York: Basic Books, 1987), pp. 147 ff.; and Neil H. Katz, "Radical Pacifism and the Contemporary American Peace Movement: The Committee for Nonviolent Action, 1957–1967" (Ph.D. dissertation, University of Maryland, 1974).

7. See SANE press release, July 17, 1957, SCPC, Scott MSS, Box 1, SANE folder.

8. Figures taken from Isserman, *If I Had a Hammer,* p. 149.

9. Albert S. Bigelow, "Why I Am Sailing into the Pacific Bomb-Test Area," *Liberation* 2, no. 11 (February 1958): 4–8.

10. See statements to court given by Bigelow, Huntington, Willoughby, and Sherwood, May 7, 1958, SCPC, Albert Bigelow MSS, Box 1.

11. On the "Golden Rule" Action, see James Peck, "Jail Is Our Home Port"; William Huntington, "If You Feel Like It"; and A. J. Muste, "Follow the Golden Rule," all in *Liberation* 3, no. 4 (June 1958): 4–8.

12. On media coverage and the public response to the "Golden Rule" action, see Muste, "Follow the Golden Rule"; Wittner, *Rebels against War,* p. 249; and Isserman, *If I Had a Hammer,* p. 154.

13. See Lawrence Scott to Sam Tyson, et al., February 17, 1958, SCPC, Scott MSS, Box 2.

14. Lawrence Scott to Ted Olson, July 22, 1958, SCPC, Scott MSS, Box 5, Cheyenne folder.

15. See Ted Olson to Lawrence Scott, July 25, 1958; Scott to Olson, July 30, 1958; Olson to Scott, August 1, 1958; Art Springer to Scott, August 4, 1958; and Scott to Springer, August 15, 1958, all at SCPC, Scott MSS, Box 5, Cheyenne folder.

16. On Cheyenne Project, see Bradford Lyttle, "Comments on the Use

of Nonviolent Obstruction at Cheyenne," 1958, SCPC, Scott MSS, Box 5, Cheyenne folder; Neil H. Katz, "Radical Pacifism and the Contemporary American Peace Movement," pp. 72–75; and Isserman, *If I Had a Hammer,* pp. 156–58.

17. Lawrence Scott to George Willoughby, A. J. Muste, Bayard Rustin, and Robert Pickus, August 28, 1958, SCPC, Scott MSS, Box 5, Cheyenne folder.

18. Lawrence Scott to George Willoughby, A. J. Muste, Robert Pickus, Lyle Tatum, and Bayard Rustin, September 6, 1958, SCPC, Scott MSS, Box 5, Cheyenne folder.

19. See author's interview with Brad Lyttle, 11/26/94.

20. While defending obstructionism, Lyttle was careful to draw the following distinction in his own position on its use at Cheyenne: "I believe nonviolent obstruction should be *allowed* at the Cheyenne demonstration, not that it should be a planned part of the program" [emphasis in original]. Bradford Lyttle, "Comments on the Use of Nonviolent Obstruction at Cheyenne," 1958, SCPC, Scott MSS, Box 5, Cheyenne folder.

21. Bradford Lyttle, "On Nonviolent Obstruction," *Liberation* 3, no. 8 (November 1958): 10–11.

22. A. J. Muste to Lawrence Scott, September 9, 1958, SCPC, Scott MSS, Box 5.

23. See A. J. Muste, "Reflections on 'Nonviolent Intervention,'" SCPC, Scott MSS, Box 5, Omaha folder.

24. See *Omaha Action Bulletin* of July 1, 1959; July 6, 1959; July 8, 1959; July 11, 1959; July 14, 1959; July 17, 1959; July 23, 1959; July 28, 1959; August 5, 1959; November 3, 1959; and December 16, 1959, all at SCPC, Scott MSS, Box 5, Omaha folder. See also Wilmer Young, "Visible Witness," in Staughton Lynd, ed., *Nonviolence in America: A Documentary History* (New York: Bobbs-Merrill, 1966), pp. 347–60.

25. On expected female roles within the family in the 1950s, see Elaine Tyler May, *Homeward Bound: American Families in the Cold War Era* (New York: Basic Books, 1988).

26. Quoted in Jhan and June Robbins, "You Are a Bad Mother," reprinted from *Redbook* (August 1960 [?]), SCPC, Scott MSS, Box 5. See also author's interview with Marjorie Swann, 4/1/91.

27. Jhan and June Robbins, "129 Ways to Get a Husband," *McCall's* 85 (January 1958): 28–29; and "Forty-Nine Ways to Make Marriage More Exciting," *Reader's Digest* 74 (January 1959): 113–14.

28. Jhan and June Robbins, "You Are a Bad Mother."

29. Marjorie Swann to Judge Robinson, July 28, 1959, reprinted in *Omaha Action Bulletin,* July 28, 1959, SCPC, Scott MSS, Box 5, Omaha folder. In the *Bulletin,* Swann's letter appears below a photograph of her four children.

30. Jhan and June Robbins, "You Are a Bad Mother."

31. See Amy Swerdlow, *Women Strike for Peace: Traditional Motherhood and Radical Politics in the 1960s* (Chicago: University of Chicago Press, 1993).

32. Isserman, *If I Had a Hammer,* p. 174.

33. On the Forum, see Robinson, *Abraham Went Out,* pp. 100–102; and Isserman, *If I Had a Hammer,* pp. 174–80.

34. See Wittner, *Rebels against War,* p. 267; and Charles DeBenedetti, *An American Ordeal: The Antiwar Movement of the Vietnam Era* (Syracuse, NY: Syracuse University Press, 1990), p. 41.

35. See "What Is SDS?" Students for a Democratic Society pamphlet, 1962, Hoover Institution, Stanford University, SDS MSS, Microfilm reel 1.

36. Author's interview with Tom Cornell, 5/6/95. See also Nancy Zaroulis and Gerald Sullivan, *Who Spoke Up?: American Protest against the War in Vietnam, 1963–1975* (New York: Doubleday and Co., 1984), p. 57.

37. Author's interview with Bradford Lyttle, 11/26/94.

38. Author's interview with Tom Cornell, 5/6/95.

39. A. J. Muste, "The Crisis in SANE: Act II," *Liberation* 5, no. 9 (November 1960): 8.

40. A public statement by the pacifist-led National Mobilization Committee to End the War in Vietnam (Mobilization or just Mobe) shows that pacifist leaders understood this implication of nonexclusion by the late 1960s: "From its earliest conception in July 1966," the statement read, "one of the prime objectives of the Mobilization was the welding together of the widest possible grouping of people who are opposed to America's brutal and brutalizing war in Vietnam. This objective was carried out with unqualified success. Despite several attempts at red-baiting, 'black-power' baiting, and other attempts to split the movement, no political tendency was excluded either from planning or participating in the [1967] April 15th Spring Mobilization. The massive popular support given to the Mobilization confirmed the wisdom of this policy. . . . The Spring Mobilization is the widest coalition of political and social forces this country has seen." ("Statement of Purpose," National Mobilization Committee to End the War in Vietnam MSS, SCPC, Box 1.)

41. Jack Newfield, "Revolt without Dogma: The Student Left," *Nation* 200, May 10, 1965: 494.

42. See, for instance, Dave Dellinger, "Nonviolence and the Black Rebellion," *Liberation* 12, no. 4 (July 1967): 3–5; and Henry Anderson, "A Case against the Drug Culture," *Liberation* 12, no. 2 (April 1967): 34–39.

43. See Meier and Rudwick, *CORE,* p. 102.

44. See ibid.

45. See "Sit-Ins: The Students Report," CORE pamphlet, May, 1960, SCPC, CORE MSS.

46. See 1961 CORE pamphlet, "Violence Follows the Freedom Riders in Alabama," SCPC, CORE MSS; and Meier and Rudwick, *CORE,* pp. 135–44.

47. Barbara Deming, a marcher who had recently joined CNVA, was moved by her experience in Albany to write a powerful book of poetry, *Prison*

Notes, incorporated with other material into *Prisons That Could Not Hold* (San Francisco: Spinsters Ink, 1985).

48. Author's interview with Brad Lyttle, 11/26/94; and Brad Lyttle letter to author, 5/18/95.

SIX

1. Jack Newfield, *A Prophetic Minority* (New York: New American Library, 1966), pp. 30–33.

2. Penina M. Glazer, "A Decade of Transition: A Study of Radical Journals of the 1940s" (Ph.D. dissertation, Rutgers University, 1970), p. ii.

3. Paul Booth interview with James Miller, quoted in James Miller, *Democracy Is in the Streets: From Port Huron to the Siege of Chicago* (New York: Simon and Schuster, 1987), p. 322. The formulation presented here builds upon the analysis in Staughton Lynd, "Marxism-Leninism and the Language of *Politics* Magazine: The First New Left . . . and the Third," in George Abbott White, ed., *Simone Weill: Interpretations of a Life* (Amherst: University of Massachusetts Press, 1981), pp. 111–35, and Maurice Isserman, *If I Had a Hammer.* See also Gregory Nevala Calvert, *Democracy from the Heart: Spiritual Values, Decentralism, and Democratic Idealism in the Movement of the 1960s* (Eugene, OR: Communitatis Press, 1991).

4. Author's interview with Tom Cornell, 5/6/95. See also Zaroulis and Sullivan, *Who Spoke Up?*, pp. 12–13.

5. See author's interview with Dave Dellinger, 5/17/95. See also Zaroulis and Sullivan, *Who Spoke Up?*, p. 20.

6. Bayard Rustin, "From Protest to Politics: The Future of the Civil Rights Movement," *Commentary* 39, no. 2 (February 1965): 25–31.

7. See Staughton Lynd, "The Freedom Schools: Concept and Organization," in Massimo Teodori, ed., *The New Left: A Documentary History* (New York: Bobbs-Merrill, 1969), 102–5. See also Clayborne Carson, *In Struggle: SNCC and the Black Awakening of the 1960s* (Cambridge, MA: Harvard University Press, 1981), 177–78.

8. Staughton Lynd, "Coalition Politics or Nonviolent Revolution?" *Liberation* 10, no. 4 (June–July 1965): 18.

9. "Response from Staughton Lynd," *Liberation* 10, no. 7 (October 1965): 29.

10. Letter to editors by Michael Harrington et al., *Liberation* 10, no. 7 (October 1965): 29.

11. Response of editors to letter from Michael Harrington et al., *Liberation* 10, no. 7 (October 1965): 29.

12. Barbara Deming, "It's a Good Life," *Liberation* 12, no. 6 (September/October 1967): 60.

13. See "CORE Hears Cries of 'Black Power,'" *New York Times,* 7/2/66; and "CORE Eliminates 'Multiracial' in Describing Its Membership," *New*

York Times, 7/6/67. See also William L. Van Deburg, *New Day in Babylon: The Black Power Movement and American Culture, 1965–1975* (Chicago: University of Chicago Press, 1992), 129–91.

14. "CORE Is Assailed by Lillian Smith," *New York Times,* 7/6/66.

15. Author's interview with Dave McReynolds, 10/16/94.

16. Author's interview with Bill Sutherland, 11/12/91.

17. James Peck, "Black Racism," *Liberation* 11, no. 7 (October 1966): 31–32.

18. Staughton Lynd, "On Black Power," *Liberation* 11, no. 5 (August 1966): 5–6.

19. Staughton Lynd, "Resistance: From Mood to Strategy," *Liberation* 12, no. 8 (November 1967): 41. See also Dave Dellinger, "Resistance: Vietnam and America," in ibid., pp. 3–7.

20. Author's interview with Dave McReynolds, 10/16/94.

21. Author's interview with Ira Sandperl, 3/13/91.

22. Author's interview with Dave Dellinger, 5/17/95.

23. Dellinger, *From Yale to Jail,* p. 283.

24. Ibid., p. 285.

25. See ibid., p. 300.

26. Dave Dellinger, "Resistance: Vietnam and America," *Liberation* 12, no. 8 (November 1967): 5–6.

27. Dave Dellinger, "Resistance," p. 7.

28. Author's interview with Dave Dellinger, 5/17/95.

29. Dave Dellinger, "Resistance," p. 7.

30. Marty Jezer, "The Yippies Are Coming!," *Liberation* 12, no. 11 (February 1968): 7–8. The spelling of "Yippies" tended to vary, not that such grammatical niceties concerned them.

31. "The Post-Competitive, Comparative Game of a Free City," *Liberation* 13, no. 3 (July/August 1968): 26–27.

32. *New York Times,* August 30, 1968. For more on the Chicago protest, see David Farber, *Chicago '68* (Chicago: University of Chicago Press, 1988).

33. See, for example, "Statement by Dave Dellinger, Chairman," March 21, 1969, SCPC, National Mobilization Committee to End the War in Vietnam MSS, Box 5.

34. Dave Dellinger, "Lessons from Chicago," *Liberation* 13, no. 5 (October 1968): 8.

35. See, for instance, the summary of a 1953 speech in which Dellinger assured a predominantly socialist audience that members of Peacemakers were not "soft" or "bourgeois" and that Peacemakers felt more affinity for "those whose understanding of society leads them to be revolutionary and not pacifist" than with "those who reject violence but can swallow the rest of the evil . . . society that surrounds us." Summary in "Third Camp Conference," published by *Labor Action,* December 14, 1953, SCPC, Peacemakers Box, p. 6.

36. Dave Dellinger, "Lessons from Chicago," p. 8.

37. Staughton Lynd, "On 'Anti-Communism,'" *Liberation* 14, no. 3 (June 1969): 3–4.

38. Carol McEldowney, "Communications: Weathermen," *Liberation* 14, no. 8 (November 1969): 45–46.

39. Dave Dellinger, "Commentary," *Liberation* 14, no. 1 (March/April 1969): 45–46.

Bibliography

BOOKS AND DISSERTATIONS CITED IN FOOTNOTES

Anderson, Jervis. *A. Philip Randolph: A Biographical Portrait*. New York: Harcourt Brace Jovanovich, 1973.

Ansbro, John J. *Martin Luther King, Jr.: The Making of a Mind*. Maryknoll, New York: Orbis Books, 1982.

Bell, Howard M. *Youth Tell Their Story: A Study of the Conditions and Attitudes of Young People in Maryland between the Ages of 16 and 24*. Washington, D.C.: American Council on Education, 1938.

Branch, Taylor. *Parting the Waters: America in the King Years, 1954–1963*. New York: Simon and Schuster, 1988.

Brax, Ralph S. *The First Student Movement: Student Activism in the United States during the 1930s*. Port Washington, New York: Kennikat Press, 1981.

Calvert, Gregory Nevala. *Democracy from the Heart: Spiritual Values, Decentralism, and Democratic Idealism in the Movement of the 1960s*. Eugene, Oregon: Communitatis Press, 1991.

Cantril, Hadley, ed. *Public Opinion, 1935–1946*. Princeton: Princeton University Press, 1951.

Carson, Clayborne. *In Struggle: SNCC and the Black Awakening of the 1960s*. Cambridge, Massachusetts: Harvard University Press, 1981.

Chappell, David L. *Inside Agitators: White Southerners in the Civil Rights Movement.* Baltimore: Johns Hopkins University Press, 1994.

Cohen, Robert. *When the Old Left Was Young: Student Radicals and America's First Mass Student Movement, 1929–1941.* New York: Oxford University Press, 1993.

Coles, Robert. *Dorothy Day: A Radical Devotion.* Reading, Massachusetts: Addison-Wesley, 1987.

Cone, James. *Martin and Malcolm and America: A Dream or a Nightmare.* Maryknoll, New York: Orbis Books, 1991.

DeBenedetti, Charles. *An American Ordeal: The Antiwar Movement of the Vietnam Era.* Syracuse: Syracuse University Press, 1990.

————. *The Peace Reform in American History.* Bloomington: Indiana University Press, 1980.

Dellinger, David. *From Yale to Jail: The Life Story of a Moral Dissenter.* New York: Pantheon Books, 1993.

Deming, Barbara. *Prisons That Could Not Hold.* San Francisco, Spinsters Ink, 1985.

Erikson, Erik. *Gandhi's Truth: On the Origins of Militant Nonviolence.* New York: W. W. Norton, 1969.

Evans, Sara. *Personal Politics: The Roots of Women's Liberation in the Civil Rights Movement and the New Left.* New York: Random House, 1980.

Fairclough, Adam. *To Redeem the Soul of America: The Southern Christian Leadership Conference and Martin Luther King, Jr.* Athens: University of Georgia Press, 1987.

Farber, David. *Chicago '68.* Chicago: University of Chicago Press, 1988.

Farmer, James. *Lay Bare the Heart: An Autobiography of the Civil Rights Movement.* New York: Arbor House, 1985.

Fischer, Louis. *The Life of Mahatma Gandhi.* New York: Harper and Bros., 1950.

Forest, James. *Love Is the Measure: A Biography of Dorothy Day.* New York: Paulist Press, 1986.

Franklin, John Hope, and Moss, Alfred A., Jr. *From Slavery to Freedom: A History of Negro Americans.* New York: Alfred A. Knopf, 1988.

Gandhi, Mohandas K. *An Autobiography, or The Story of My Experiments with Truth.* Ahmedabad: Navijivan Publishing House, 1956.

Garrow, David J. *Bearing the Cross: Martin Luther King, Jr., and the Southern Christian Leadership Conference.* New York: Random House, 1988.

————. ed. *The Walking City: The Montgomery Bus Boycott, 1955–1956,* vol. 7 in series entitled *Martin Luther King, Jr., and the Civil Rights Movement.* New York: Carlson Publishing, 1989.

Genovese, Eugene D. *Roll, Jordan, Roll: The World the Slaves Made.* New York: Vintage Books, 1974.

Gitlin, Todd. *The Sixties: Years of Hope, Days of Rage.* New York: Bantam Books, 1989.

Glazer, Penina M. "A Decade of Transition: A Study of Radical Journals of the 1940s." Ph.D. dissertation, Rutgers University, 1970.

Gutman, Herbert G. *The Black Family in Slavery and Freedom, 1750–1925.* New York: Pantheon Books, 1976.

Hentoff, Nat. *Peace Agitator: The Story of A. J. Muste.* New York: Macmillan, 1963.

Horne, Gerald. *Communist Front: The Civil Rights Congress, 1946–1956.* East Rutherford, New Jersey: Fairleign Dickinson University Press, 1988.

Houser, George. *No One Can Stop the Rain: Glimpses of Africa's Liberation Struggle.* New York: Pilgrim Press, 1989.

Isserman, Maurice. *If I Had a Hammer: The Death of the Old Left and the Birth of the New Left.* New York: Basic Books, 1987.

Katz, Neil H. "Radical Pacifism and the Contemporary American Peace Movement: The Committee for Nonviolent Action, 1957–1967." Ph.D. dissertation, University of Maryland, 1974.

Keim, Albert N., and Stoltzfus, Grant M. *The Politics of Conscience: The Historic Peace Churches and America at War, 1917–1955.* Scottdale, Pennsylvania: Herald Press, 1988.

Kelley, Robin D. G. *Hammer and Hoe: Alabama Communists during the Great Depression.* Chapel Hill: University of North Carolina Press, 1990.

King, Martin Luther, Jr. *Stride toward Freedom: The Montgomery Story.* New York: Harper and Brothers, 1958.

Klejment, Anne. *Dorothy Day and the Catholic Worker: A Bibliography.* New York: Garland, 1986.

Lynd, Robert S. and Lynd, Helen Merrell. *Middletown: A Study in Modern American Culture.* New York: Harcourt, Brace, and World, 1929.

Lynd, Staughton, ed. *Nonviolence in America: A Documentary History.* New York: Bobbs-Merrill, 1966.

May, Elaine Tyler. *Homeward Bound: American Families in the Cold War Era.* New York: Basic Books, 1988.

Mayer, Peter, ed. *The Pacifist Conscience.* New York: Holt, Rinehart, and Winston, 1966.

Meier, August, and Rudwick, Elliot. *CORE: A Study in the Civil Rights Movement.* New York: Oxford University Press, 1973.

Miller, James. *Democracy Is in the Streets: From Port Huron to the Siege of Chicago.* New York: Simon and Schuster, 1987.

Morris, Aldon D. *The Origins of the Civil Rights Movement: Black Communities Organizing for Change.* New York: The Free Press, 1984.

National Service Board for Religious Objectors. *Directory of Civilian Public Service: May, 1941 to March, 1947.* Washington, D.C.: National Service Board for Religious Objectors, 1947.

Nelson, Jacquelyn S. *Indiana Quakers Confront the Civil War.* Indianapolis: Indiana Historical Society, 1991.

Newfield, Jack. *A Prophetic Minority.* New York: New American Library, 1966.

Peck, Jim. *We Who Would Not Kill.* New York: Lyle Stuart, 1958.

Pells, Richard H. *The Liberal Mind in a Conservative Age: American Intellectuals in the 1940s and 1950s.* Middletown, Connecticut: Wesleyan University Press, 1989.

Pfeffer, Paula A. *A. Philip Randolph, Pioneer of the Civil Rights Movement.* Baton Rouge: Louisiana State University Press, 1990.

Robinson, Joann Ooiman. *Abraham Went Out: A Biography of A. J. Muste.* Philadelphia: Temple University Press, 1981.

Schlissel, Lillian, ed. *Conscience in America: A Documentary History of Conscientious Objection in America, 1757–1967.* New York: E. P. Dutton and Co., 1968.

Smith, Kenneth L., and Zepp, Ira G. *Search for the Beloved Community: The Thinking of Martin Luther King, Jr.* Valley Forge, Pennsylvania: Judson Press, 1980.

Stampp, Kenneth M. *The Peculiar Institution: Slavery in the Ante-Bellum South.* New York: Knopf, 1956.

Swerdlow, Amy. *Women Strike for Peace: Traditional Motherhood and Radical Politics in the 1960s.* Chicago: University of Chicago Press, 1993.

Teodori, Massimo, ed. *The New Left: A Documentary History.* New York: Bobbs-Merrill, 1969.

Trachtenberg, Alan. *The Incorporation of America: Culture and Society in the Gilded Age.* New York: Hill and Wang, 1982.

Troester, Rosalie Riegle, ed. *Voices from the Catholic Worker.* Philadelphia: Temple University Press, 1993.

Unger, Irwin. *The Movement: A History of the American New Left, 1959–1972.* New York: Harper and Row, 1974.

Van Deburg, William L. *New Day in Babylon: The Black Power Movement and American Culture, 1965–1975.* Chicago: University of Chicago Press, 1992.

White, George Abbott, ed. *Simone Weill: Interpretations of a Life.* Amherst: University of Massachusetts Press, 1981.

Wiebe, Robert H. *The Search for Order, 1877–1920.* New York: Hill and Wang, 1967.

Wittner, Lawrence S. *Rebels against War: The American Peace Movement, 1933–1983.* Philadelphia: Temple University Press, 1984.

Wreszin, Michael. *A Rebel in Defense of Tradition: The Life and Politics of Dwight Macdonald.* New York: Basic Books, 1994.

Zaroulis, Nancy, and Sullivan, Gerald. *Who Spoke Up?: American Protest against the War in Vietnam, 1963–1975.* New York: Doubleday and Co., 1984.

Index

167n.47; in Lawrence textile strike, 23; leadership of radical pacifists, xiv; and *Liberation* magazine, 85–86, 98, 116, 123, 126; Lyttle supported by, 108–10, 123; on March on Washington Movement, 26; Marxist period of, 24; Musteism, 24; in Nevada Action, 99, 101, 102; and the New Left, 111–12, 116; nonexclusionism supported by, 115–16, 123; on nonviolent direct action, 53, 98; on obstructionism, 108–9; in Omaha Action, 110; in Peacemakers, 60, 61, 73–75; on peacetime draft, 63; and the Peace Walks, 121; photograph in 1958, *25;* and Randolph's draft resistance campaign, 64–65; and Randolph's proposed civil disobedience campaign, 34–35; resigning from War Resisters League, 82; role in Fellowship of Reconciliation, 23, 24; Rustin converted to pacifism by, 30; Rustin expelled from Fellowship of Reconciliation by, 82; on SANE's demise, 115; and Spring Mobilization to End the War in Vietnam, 136; in tax resistance campaign, 66; on total dedication to Peacemakers, 62; Union Eight supported by, 27; in Vietnam War protests, 128, 129, 134, 135; and younger radicals, 111–12, 116, 139–40. *See also* Fellowship of Reconciliation

Musteism, 24

NAACP, Farmer on, 22
National Committee for Conscientious Objectors, 79

National Coordinating Committee to End the War in Vietnam (NCCEWVN), 134–35
National Mobilization Committee to End the War in Vietnam, 141, 146–47, 170n.40
Nelson, Wally, 55
Nevada Action, 99, 101, 102
Newark Ashram, 6
Newfield, Jack, 116, 125
New Left, 111–14; influences on, 126; Muste as bridge between Old Left and, 116; National Mobilization Committee to End the War in Vietnam, 141, 146–47, 170n.40; the new radicalism, 124–28; radical pacifism's influence on, 126–28; Student Peace Union, 112–13, 126; Third World revolutionaries romanticized by, 136. *See also* Student Nonviolent Coordinating Committee; Students for a Democratic Society
New Mobilization Committee to End the War in Vietnam, 151
new radicalism, 124–28
Niebuhr, Reinhold: Christian Realism of, 5, 93; civil disobedience opposed by, 35; and Houser, 20; King influenced by, 93; on pacifism, 5; Social Gospel rejected by, 4–5; Union Eight denounced by, 1, 2
Nixon, E. D., 90
Nixon, Richard, 152
nonexclusionism, 115–16, 123, 170n.40
nonviolence: in Fellowship of Reconciliation organizing, 90; in Houser's plan for a political movement, 21; King and, 92–95; in KPFA programming,

nonviolence (*cont.*)
60; Smiley and Rustin advocating in Montgomery boycott, 91–92; as tactic of radical pacifists, xiv, 35, 46. *See also* nonviolent direct action
Non-Violent Action Against Nuclear Weapons (NVAANW), 101
nonviolent direct action (NVDA): in antiwar movement and Civil Rights movement, 123; March on Washington Movement endorsing, 34; as method for revolutionizing society, 21; Muste on, 53, 98; obstructionism, 105, 107, 108–9, 110, 169n.20; as radical pacifist tactic, 35, 153; Randolph's retreat from, 35
November Mobilization, 151–52
nuclear weapons, 99–111: atomic bomb, 47–48, 51, 68, 100; Einstein-Russell Appeal, 83, 84; "Golden Rule" action, 102–4, 109; hydrogen bomb, 68, 83–84, 99; Nevada Action, 99, 101, 102; Non-Violent Action Against Nuclear Weapons, 101; Omaha Action, 110–11; Peace Walks, 121–22; Polaris Action, 113–14. *See also* SANE
NVDA. *See* nonviolent direct action

obstructionism, 105, 107, 108–9, 110, 169n.20
Ochs, Phil, 143
Oglesby, Carl, 116
Old Left: Dellinger using rhetoric of, 149; mass movements understood by, 128; Muste as bridge between New Left and, 116; the new radicalism compared

with, 125–28; radical pacifists rejecting, 125–26. *See also* Marxists
Olson, Ted: in Cheyenne Project, 105–7; Muste on, 108, 109
Omaha Action, 110–11
Orangeburg, South Carolina, boycott, 89–90
Otsuka, James, 107
Oxford Pledge, 6–7

Pacifica radio (KPFA), 59–60
pacifism: and America First Committee, 7–8; and Communist front groups, 69; Historic Peace churches embracing, 8–9; isolationism supplanting, 7–8; leadership urging Union Eight to compromise, 11; Niebuhr on, 5; 1940 as bad year for, 6; the Oxford Pledge, 6–7; popularity of in 1930s, 6; radical pacifists and traditional, 41, 46; traditional pacifists shrinking from confrontation, 27. *See also* conscientious objectors; radical pacifists
Palisades Pool (New Jersey) desegregation, 68
Parks, Rosa, 91
Parris, Robert (Robert Moses), 133, 134, *135*
participatory democracy, 40, 125, 153
Pauling, Linus, 83
Peace Churches. *See* Historic Peace Churches
Peacemaker Mutual Aid Fund, 79
Peacemakers, 60–67; the Baden Action, 71–73; "Call for a Conference on More Disciplined and Revolutionary Pacifist Activity," 61; Chicago conference of 1948, 61; divergences in during Cold